M000046176

Trailside's
Hints & Tips
For Outdoor
Adventure

Trailside's Hints & Tips For Outdoor Adventure

By the Editors of
BACKPACKER
Magazine

Edited by John Viehman
Host of "Trailside: Make Your Own Adventure"
and Executive Editor of **BACKPACKER** Magazine

Rodale Press, Emmaus, Pennsylvania

Copyright © 1993 by Rodale Press, Inc.

All rights reserved. No part of this publication may be reproduced or transmitted in any form or by any means, electronic or mechanical, including photocopy, recording, or any other information storage and retrieval system, without the written permission of the publisher.

BACKPACKER Magazine is a registered trademark of Rodale Press, Inc.

TRAILSIDE™ is a registered trademark of New Media, Inc.

Printed in the United States of America on acid-free ∞ paper

Compiled by Laurence Wiland
Editor: John Viehman
Managing editor: Tom Shealey

Cover designer: Stan Green
Interior designer: John Pepper
Copy editor: Nancy Humes
Cover photographer: Mitch Mandel

"Bear Bagging Your Food" (pp. 81–85) reprinted from *Hiking: A Celebration of the Sport and the World's Best Places to Enjoy It*. Text copyright © 1992 by Cindy Ross. Copyright © 1992 by Bryon Preiss/Richard Ballantine, Inc.

If you have any questions or comments regarding this book, please write:
Rodale Press
Book Readers' Service
33 East Minor Street
Emmaus, PA 18098

ISBN 0-87596-170-3 paperback

Distributed in the book trade by St. Martin's Press

2   4   6   8   10   9   7   5   3   1   paperback

CONTENTS

INTRODUCTION

Everyone has a mental image of the typical wily woodsman. He's a grizzled character, sort of in the Daniel Boone mold. He usually sports a healthy growth of beard, wears a flannel shirt, an old hat, and is never without his well-worn hiking stick. Ask a question about anything from staying warm when the snow falls to where the deer eat their evening meal and he knows the answers. Nature and time were his teachers.

This book is your shortcut. In these chapters you'll find enough time-tested hints and tips to fill the heads of a dozen Davy Crocketts. Everything from medical matters to hiking in extreme hot or cold temperatures to finding clean drinking water to backpacking in foreign lands—it's all here. So read on, then find an old hat that suits you and grab your hiking stick. Whether you're hiking the Appalachian Trail, snowshoeing in Glacier National Park or sea kayaking along the Baja peninsula, you're on your way to becoming a full-fledged wily woodsman.

John Viehman
Host, "Trailside: Make Your Own Adventure" and Executive Editor, *Backpacker* Magazine

chapter one:
CHOOSING THE RIGHT PLACE TO GO

Ahh, vacation. You've finally got that glorious week or weekend off, and you're itching to hit the trail.

You start the best outdoor trips indoors, browsing through guidebooks, looking at maps, and making phone calls. The best guidebooks are like good friends who tell you about special places, then send you on your way, never stealing from the surprise of the journey. Most outfitters keep their shelves stocked with lots of guidebooks for people with the time for adventure. And a good map is . . . like a good map. There's nothing that compares with the functional clarity of a well-executed map, one easier to read than a book but that holds more information than can be packed into 100 pages of text.

A visit to your local library might turn up excellent planning resources, and this listing of outdoor book and map publishers will also help you plan your next (or first!) adventure.

BOOK PUBLISHERS

Adirondack Mountain Club, R.R. 3, Box 3055, Lake George, NY 12845; (518) 668-4447. Regions: the forest preserve of New York, the Adirondacks, and the Catskills. Subjects: hiking and canoeing guides, natural history, how-to, and literature. Specialty: hiking guides to the forest preserve of New York.

Appalachian Mountain Club Books, 5 Joy St., Boston, MA 02108; (617) 523-0636. Regions: traditionally northeastern United States, but also the Southeast and Canada. Subjects:

hiking and climbing guides, natural history, and how-to. Specialty: hiking guides.

Appalachian Trail Conference, P.O. Box 807, Harpers Ferry, WV 25425; (304) 535-6331. Region: eastern United States. Subjects: hiking guides and natural history. Specialty: Appalachian trails.

Backcountry Bookstore, P.O. Box 191, Snohomish, WA 98290; (206) 568-8722. Subjects: outdoor guides, how-to, and literature. Catalogs available. More than 1,600 book titles.

Backcountry Publications, P.O. Box 175, Woodstock, VT 05091; (800) 245-4151. Region: predominantly the Northeast. Subjects: hiking, canoeing, walking, ski touring, and bicycling guides, and how-to. Specialty: hiking guides.

Chessler Books, P.O. Box 399, Kittredge, CO 80457; (800) 654-8502; (303) 670-0093 in CO and outside the U.S. Regions: United States and international. Subjects: mountaineering, trail guides, how-to, literature, adventure travel, maps, and videos. More than 1,500 new and 2,000 used books. Catalogs available on each subject. One of the best sources of hard-to-find, first-edition, and antique mountaineering literature.

Globe Pequot, 6 Business Park Rd., Box 833, Old Saybrook, CT 06475; (800) 243-0495. Regions: United States and international. Subjects: hiking and bicycling guides, how-to, natural history, and literature. More than 40 titles on outdoor recreation.

ICS Books, 1370 E. 86th Place, Merrilville, IN 46410; (800) 541-7323; FAX (800) 336-8834. Regions: United States and international. Subjects: how-to and literature. Specialty: novice outdoor skills.

Kelsey Publishing, 456 E. 100 North, Provo, UT 84606; (801) 374-1747. Regions: Utah and Colorado Plateau, and international. Subjects: hiking and climbing guides. Specialty: hiking guides to Utah. Price list available.

The Mountaineers, 1011 SW Klickitat Way, Suite 107, Seattle, WA 98134; (800) 553-4453; (206) 223-6303 in WA; FAX (206) 223-6306. More than half of the 160+ titles are guidebooks. Regions: United States and international. Subjects: hiking, canoeing, kayaking, and regional guides; natural history, how-to, adventure travel, current affairs, and literature. Specialty: Pacific Northwest trail guides.

REI, P.O. Box 1700, Sumner, WA 98352; (800) 426-4840. With more than 37 locations across the country, REI is an excellent regional resource. "Outdoor advisors" (ask for them when you call) are pleased to provide recommendations for books covering particular areas. Books are not listed in REI's mail-order catalogs.

Sierra Club Books, 730 Polk St., San Francisco, CA 94109; (415) 923-5500. Regions: United States and international. Subjects: hiking, climbing, and regional guides; how-to, pictorial, adventure travel, natural history, literature, and current affairs.

Stackpole Books, P.O. Box 1831, Cameron and Kelker streets, Harrisburg, PA 17105; (800) 732-3669; FAX (717) 234-1359. Regions: United States and Canada. Subjects: natural history and how-to.

Touchstone Press, P.O. Box 81, Beaverton, OR 97075; (800) 877-2684. Regions: the Northwest and California. Subjects: hiking, mountain biking, and nature guides. Specialty: hiking guides.

Whitecap Books, 1086 W. 3rd St., N. Vancouver, BC, Canada V7P 3J6; (604) 980-9852; FAX (604) 980-8197. Region: Canada. Subjects: hiking and boating guides, natural history, and pictorial. Specialty: British Columbia.

Wilderness Press, 2440 Bancroft Way, Berkeley, CA 94704; (800) 443-7227; FAX (510) 548-1355. Regions: the western United States and Hawaii. Subjects: hiking guides, how-to, natural history, and literature. Specialty: 32 guides of Sierra Nevada.

MAP PUBLISHERS

Adirondack Mountain Club, address above. The Adirondack Mountain Club (ADK) publishes seven four-color topos to accompany its guidebooks. Each map measures 33 inches by 20 inches.

Appalachian Mountain Club, address above. AMC's 10 maps cover the Appalachian and White mountains of Maine, New Hampshire, and Massachusetts. Of particular interest is Brad Washburn's excellent map of Mount Washington. The maps are available on paper or waterproof plastic.

Custom Correct Maps, Little River Enterprises, 3492 Little River Rd., Port Angeles, WA 98362; (206) 457-5667. Tom Shindler, a former Olympic National Park ranger, began making maps because "anything of interest is always on the border of two quads, one of which you don't have." He produces a highly accurate 16-map series based on USGS 15-minute topos, covering all of the trails in Olympic National Park and wilderness areas of the Olympic National Forest. An index map and order form are available on request.

DeLorme Mapping Co., P.O. Box 298, Freeport, ME 04032; (800) 227-1656. DeLorme produces a topographic state atlas and gazetteer series that includes New York, Pennsylvania, Virginia, Tennessee, Wisconsin, Washington, Northern California, southcentral California, Alaska, Minnesota, Oregon, Illinois, Colorado, Idaho, Maine, New Hampshire, Vermont, North Carolina, Florida, Ohio, and Michigan. The gazetteer section of each atlas contains 1,200 to 2,000 listings, including state and national parks and forests, trails, campgrounds, and natural features. Maps are based on the USGS 7½-minute series topos. DeLorme also publishes the Maine Geographic Series, a collection of hiking, biking, canoeing, and nature maps for that state.

Green Trails Maps, P.O. Box 1932, Bothell, WA 98041; (206) 485-9144. During the 20 years Walt Locke has updated USGS topographical maps, he's created 100 maps covering Washington's Cascades and Olympics and 15 maps of the Oregon Cascades south to Mount Jefferson. The conveniently sized 12-inch by 18-inch maps are smaller than USGS topos. The trails and roads are clearly marked, and an index of adjoining maps is printed on the back.

Raven Maps and Images, 34 N. Central Ave., Medford, OR 97501; (800) 237-0798; FAX (503) 773-6834. A map-lover's delight, these 26 beautiful shaded-relief and elevation-tinted wall maps cover Alaska, Hawaii, and New England; also Yosemite, the central Sierra, Crater Lake, Mount Mazama, and additional national parks. Raven also produces a series of striking computer-generated maps of the Rockies, California-Nevada, West Virginia, Texas, Hawaii, and Mount St. Helens.

Tom Harrison Cartography, 333 Bellam Blvd., San Rafael, CA 94901; (415) 456-7940; FAX (415) 456-7940. This former California state park ranger produces six-color, shaded-relief topographical maps of California's state and national parks, wilderness areas, national forests and recreation areas, and Washington's Mount Rainier. Harrison begins with USGS topos, eliminates unnecessary details, highlights trails, and adds shadows that create a strong impression of the landform relief.

Trails Illustrated, P.O. Box 3610, Evergreen, CO 80439; (800) 962-1643; (303) 670-3457 in CO; FAX (303) 670-3644. This firm offers over 75 maps: 44 Colorado maps, a 12-map Utah series, and 20 national park maps. Each map lists hiking, backcountry, and trip-planning information, and most include interpretive highlights such as wildlife, history, geology, and archaeology. The maps are based on USGS topos and are updated prior to each annual or biannual reprinting. They're printed on a tearproof, waterproof, paperlike plastic.

U.S. Geological Survey, Distribution Branch, Box 25286, Federal Center, Bldg. 810, Denver, CO 80225; (303) 236-7477. Mail orders accepted. USGS sales counters are located in 14 cities throughout the nation.

Wilderness Press, address above. Wilderness Press's 16 maps of the Sierra Nevada and others of popular recreation areas in California present an almost overwhelming amount of information. The maps are revised frequently, and most are available on tearproof, waterproof plastic.

For more detailed planning, your best single source is the local headquarters of the agency that manages the land you'll be visiting. Explain the kind of trip you want and any special interests you might want to pursue, such as fishing, climbing, wildlife watching, or photography. In addition to brochures, maps, trail guides, and other current information, these folks will provide warnings of unusual or temporary hazards or changes in roads, trails, boundaries, and access.

You'll want all the maps you can get your hands on, especially those seemingly useless ones found on the counters at visitor centers; the ones that show things like picnic spots, routes for nature walks, picnic areas, access roads, designated campgrounds near parking lots, and public swimming sites. You can use these resources to find the kind of outdoor experience you have in mind (or to avoid the crowds that flock to certain spots).

A listing of state parks, forests, and wildlife management areas is available by calling the state office of tourism or the central office of the state park system. For addresses of local federal lands headquarters, contact:

U.S. Bureau of Land Management, Dept. of the Interior, 1849 C St. NW, Washington, DC 20240; (202) 208-4200; (202) 208-5717 for publications.

U.S. Fish and Wildlife Service, Dept. of the Interior, 1849 C St. NW, Mailstop 130 ARLSQ, Washington, DC 20240; (703) 358-1711. Ask for "National Wildlife Refuges: A Visitor's Guide."

U.S. Forest Service, Dept. of Agriculture, 14th St. and Independence Ave. SW, Washington, DC 20250; (202) 205-1760. Ask for "A Guide to Your National Forests."

U.S. National Park Service, Dept. of the Interior, P.O. Box 37127, Washington, DC 20013; (202) 208-4747. Ask for "Guide and Map: National Parks of the United States."

The Sierra Club publishes a valuable eight-pamphlet public-lands series with the following titles: "Endangered Species and Their Habitats," "National Park System," "National Wilderness Preservation System," "National Wildlife Refuge System," "National Forest System," "National Trails System," "National Wild and Scenic Rivers System," and "Bureau of Land Management." Contact: Sierra Club, Information Services, 730 Polk St., San Francisco, CA 94109; (415) 923-5660.

chapter two:
THE FINE ART OF PACKING

Now that you've got your eye on a trail, it's time to pack. Beginners invariably bring too much of all the wrong stuff. Veterans have an internal checklist created from their experiences. Here is a pretrip list of things to do.

• Clean wool garments in a bathtub or a large sink with mild liquid soap and cold water. Instead of scrubbing, squeeze and massage the garments to distribute soap and loosen dirt. Keep changing the rinse water until it runs clear. Roll the items in a towel to absorb the excess moisture, and lay them flat to air dry.
• Don't dry-clean Gore-Tex or other waterproof, breathable garments. Dry-cleaning solvents break down the fabric's water-repellent qualities, causing leaks. Instead, machine or hand wash with a powdered detergent in cold water with no bleach. Rinse on a double rinse cycle and drip dry. Although there are many soaps on the market for cleaning Gore-Tex fabrics, W. L. Gore & Associates doesn't endorse any product.
• If you plan to sleep on an air mattress, inflate it and check for leaks and faulty valves. If you find a hole, repair it with a mattress repair kit. On the trail, ripstop nylon repair tape works well in an emergency, but it's always wise to carry a patch kit.
• Machine wash fleece and pile garments and tumble dry on low heat. To minimize "pilling" that occurs with these fabrics after extensive wear and repeated washings, wash on the gentle cycle and add a small amount of fabric softener. Brushing with a soft-bristle brush while the garment is drying also helps reduce pilling.
• If you use a foam sleeping pad, take it out on the lawn

and wash it with mild soap and a sponge or soft cloth. Air dry it thoroughly before storing.

• When cleaning your stove, be sure to follow the manufacturer's instructions. Oil the movable parts and remove any carbon buildup. Check gaskets and O-rings for dryness or cracking, and replace if necessary. A bit of olive oil rubbed into a dry gasket or ring may prolong its life.

• Test your water filter. Clean it thoroughly, and replace or repair worn parts. Even if you depend on a filter, pack some form of chemical purification (iodine based) as a backup, just in case.

• Run the zippers on all your equipment and clothing (raingear, jackets, sleeping bag, backpack, and tent doors). To smooth zippers and preserve their life, clean with a toothbrush and wax lightly with paraffin. Many top-line manufacturers will repair faulty zippers free of charge, but the process may take three to six weeks, so check them out in advance.

• If you'll be camping in bear country and have to hang your food, check your 50 feet of rope and your food stuffsacks for frays and holes.

• Put together an emergency repair kit containing clevis pins, quick-release buckles, spare straps, stove parts, wire, ripstop nylon tape, and duct tape. Don't forget an air-mattress patch kit, if appropriate.

• Review your first-aid skills, and take a CPR or basic first-aid refresher course (check with your local Red Cross). Read up on hiking-specific ailments, such as hypothermia, dehydration, heat exhaustion, and heatstroke. Pack a good first-aid book with your kit. Prepare your mind as well as your gear.

• Plan to carry a whistle so you can signal for help if there's an emergency.

• Pack lighter, not heavier. Many inexperienced hikers try to carry more weight than is comfortable or safe. The result can be a less than pleasant trip or a pulled muscle. A good rule of thumb is to carry roughly one-fifth to one-quarter of your body weight. You can increase the weight to as much as one-third of your weight as you get stronger.

• Trim away ounces. Look at each piece of gear and ask yourself if there's a lighter item that can replace it. Or can you make that particular piece of gear lighter? Ounces add up to pounds. Trim extra-wide borders off maps. Cut the handle off your toothbrush. Trim unused pockets, cuffs, and belt loops off spare clothing. Use a plastic spoon and cup instead of metal ones.

- Bring a watch so you can keep an eye on the time and plan ahead. If the sky becomes overcast and the sun is obscured, darkness may catch you still on the trail. You don't want to be searching for your camp or a campsite in the dark.
- Plan to take a hiking staff, for several reasons. On rocky terrain, it serves as a third leg for better balance. When stepping over rocks or logs, you can poke around for snakes. You can use it to flick limbs and branches off the trail. It can be a third leg for stream crossings and substitute as a rest for your backpack when no trees are around.
- Take along a large garbage bag for its multitude of uses: Protect your down vest or sleeping bag with it when crossing streams; cut it open and use it as a dry emergency floor if your tent floor gets wet; slit it down one side and use it as a pack cover in the rain; slip it over your pack at night to keep dew off; cut out neck and armholes, and make an emergency poncho; use it as a liner inside your pack to keep gear dry.
- If you're using iodine to treat water, number your water bottles to easily keep track of which one was last treated.
- Scratch half-cup measuring marks on the inside of your cook pot and cup. This makes food preparation easier and prevents measuring mistakes on the trail.
- Get out your camera and shoot a test roll of film before you hit the trail. Make sure your meter, shutter, and film advance work properly. If you came across some new techniques since your last trip, experiment before you leave home. And don't forget to check the batteries.
- Try out new backcountry meals at home. Note how much fuel it takes to prepare them and how well they satisfy your taste and bulk requirements. Also, put together a fresh spice kit for the trail.
- If you'll be fishing and your reel has been sitting in the closet, straighten your line before you make that first cast. Get a friend to hold the reel and line tight. Hold the other end of the line with one hand. With a small piece of chamois cloth or leather between the fingers of your other hand (to prevent friction burns), pinch the line and rub vigorously up and down until you feel the heat through the cloth. Keep the line taut as you work your way through the entire spool. If you can't rub out most of the kinks, it's time for new line.
- Prepare for the worst. Always carry enough clothing for the worst possible weather that could occur during the time of year you're hiking. Don't rely on optimistic weather reports to determine what you pack.

LOADING AN EXTERNAL FRAME PACK

Put the heaviest gear on top. The weighty stuff—stove, cook kit, bulk foods, storm gear, water bottles, etc.—goes in the upper compartment and top side-pockets. Keep the heaviest items close to your back. Store fuel bottles and water bottles in separate pockets to avoid contamination. The tent lashes on top behind the extender bar. Odd-shaped cargo fits under the top lid.

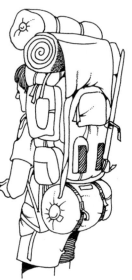

Pack midweight gear in the middle. Stow clothing, personal gear, headlamps, maps, compass, compact camera, and the like in the center compartment and lower side-pockets.

Lash long items to the frame. Tie your fly-rod case, camera tripod, and long tent poles to the sides of the frame, or shove them into tunnels behind the side-pockets. An ax or ice ax will fit into the pack's loop carrier.

Light, bulky equipment goes near the back of the pack. Lash your sleeping bag to the open area below the main packbag. Always line its stuffsack with a plastic bag—after hiking all day in the rain, you'll be glad you did. Consider

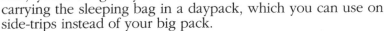

carrying the sleeping bag in a daypack, which you can use on side-trips instead of your big pack.

LOADING AN INTERNAL FRAME PACK

For easier traveling on hiking trails, pack heavy items up high for comfort. Stuff clothing around them so they won't shift. Women generally should opt for a more central positioning of heavy items.

Lighter, easily stuffed gear goes in the middle. Lightweight gear goes up high and down the back of the inside of the pack to hold the heavy items in place. Try to avoid "hinges"— soft spots in the load where the pack body flops over.

Put your sleeping bag (and perhaps some clothing, if there's room) in the bottom compartment. For best balance when walking rough terrain, pack the heaviest items lower and close to your back.

Lash odd-shaped items such as tent poles, fly rods, and avalanche shovels on the outside, using the side compressor straps and/or accessory straps on the outside of the backpack.

chapter three:
WHAT YOU MUST KNOW ABOUT WATER

Hot and dusty, flushed with the romance of the wild out-doors, you hold your cup beneath a clear-blue waterfall so cold it numbs your fingers. "Just like the mountain men," you think as cup meets lips. Ahh, nature's nectar, flowing down from the high country, where it's chilled by snow and ice and long winters. Taking your first sip, you toast the good life.

If you're lucky, you arise the following morning and start your day with a smile and breakfast. But if your water was alive—contaminated with all sorts of nasties you couldn't see—you could start with a squat and some unsavory gut wrenching. A carefree drink from what appears to be clean, mountain water, even in the most remote, pristine wilderness, can teach you an uncomfortable lesson: What you can't see *can* hurt you.

Three types of microcritters could temporarily be taking up residence in your water bottle.

Cysts. These hard-shelled, single-celled parasitic protozoa are the largest fluvial microorganisms, ranging in size from 5 to 15 microns. (A micron, one-millionth of a meter, equals .0000394 inch. The period at the end of this sentence measures a whopping 500 to 600 microns in diameter.) The ubiquitous Giardia cyst (see page 18) is responsible for most waterborne illness in the United States. *E. histolystica,* the rascal responsible for amoebic dysentery, occurs infrequently in this country. *Cryptosporidium,* unknown as a cause of human illness until 1976, is becoming an increasingly common cause of gastrointestinal upset.

Bacteria. There are a wide variety of bacteria, and most are smaller than protozoa (.2 to 10 microns). A few notorious offenders: *E. coli* comes from fecal contamination, and it gives you the trots; *Klebsiella pneumoniae* causes pneumonia; the various transmutations of salmonella can cause fever, food poisoning, and typhoid fever; shigella is another cause of dysentery; staphylococcus and streptococcus both cause big, painful, pus-filled boils.

Viruses. These are the smallest (.004 to 0.1 micron), least pervasive waterborne fauna, but are arguably the most dangerous. Viruses cause polio and hepatitis A and B (you can die from hepatitis B). Coxsackie and ECHO (enteric cytopathogenic human orphan) viruses are often asymptomatic but can cause diarrhea, flu, fever, and colds. Norwalk and Rota viruses can also cause diarrhea. An interesting note on these last four viruses comes from Dr. James Alexander of the federal Centers for Disease Control and Prevention in Atlanta, Georgia: "You are more likely to get them from your buddy than from backcountry water." Viruses currently pose little danger in the surface water throughout most of the United States and Canada.

The problem of living organisms aside, widespread disagreement remains regarding chemical pollutants in backcountry water. Some scientists say that since backpackers consume such small quantities of water for short periods of time, there's little threat. Others warn that even minimum exposure to chemicals is cause for concern. Common surface-water pollutants include diesel fuel, pesticides, fertilizers, and heavy metals from mines. Beware of any water that is discolored or has an odor.

There's no practical way to know if the water at your feet contains harmful microorganisms or pollutants. Backcountry water sources are living communities susceptible to sudden change, and the number of organisms can surge without apparent cause. The water might be safe one day but harmful the next or might be safe if drawn from one location, yet unsafe 20 yards downstream.

The prudent backpacker's only choice is to purify *all* drinking water by either killing or removing the organisms. You have three options.

1) Boiling. There was a time when a five-minute boil was recommended for making water safe. Nowadays, it's accepted that merely bringing water to a rolling boil will do, since even the lower temperatures required to make water boil at high elevations are adequate to kill Giardia, vegetative bacteria, and viruses. Even so, the inconvenience of setting up a stove and lugging extra fuel often makes this option impractical. The boiling points for high-country elevations are:

Sea level:	212° F (100° C)
5,000 ft.:	203° F (95° C)
10,000 ft.:	194° F (90° C)
14,000 ft.:	187° F (86° C)

2) Chemical treatment. In days of yore, the preferred way to treat backcountry water was with Halazone tablets, which release chlorine similar to household bleach. But chlorine isn't a panacea. Scientists discovered that it reacts with other organic materials in the water, which reduces its effectiveness. Halazone has a shelf life of only a few months if it's stored at 80° F or hotter. Within two days of opening the bottle and exposing the tablets to air, the potency is reduced, creating a hazard to the user. If that isn't enough reason to stop using chlorine, it can combine with certain organic materials to form carcinogens called trihalomethanes. It's no surprise, then, that iodine has replaced chlorine in many a pack.

Whether in tablet or crystal form, iodine is light and easy to use, though effectiveness depends on dosage concentration, the amount of time between adding iodine and drinking the water, water temperature and pH. The odd odor and flavor of iodized water make drinking it an acquired taste, so some people add flavored drink mixes to improve palatability. (Pregnant women and people with thyroid problems shouldn't ingest iodine.)

Tablets: One of the most common brand names is Potable Aqua, which comes in a tablet. It has a shelf life of five years if unopened and stored at room temperature but rapidly loses its effectiveness once opened, as do any iodine tablets. Store the tablets in an airtight bottle while on the trail. The dose is one tablet per quart of clear water at room temperature (above 50° F). Wait 15 minutes before drinking. Cloudy water or cold water requires an additional tablet and a one-hour wait.

Crystals: Iodine also comes in a crystalline, or elemental, form. The Polar Equipment Co. makes the Polar Pure kit, which consists of a glass bottle containing a small amount of crystalline iodine, a particle trap to keep the settled crystals in the bottle, and a small thermometer on the side of the bottle with a graph that indicates when the water is safe to drink. More detailed directions are fused to the bottle so they won't rub off or be left at home. Shelf life is indefinite.

One of the newest iodine-treatment methods is a release-on-demand purifier from Water Technologies Corp. Water passes through a mesh "filter" containing iodine resin, releasing iodine only when there are microorganisms present. If pure water is poured through the filter, no iodine is released. Before drinking, you must wait three minutes for the iodine to work in water at room temperature and half an hour in water near the freezing point. The problem is in determining when the iodine content has been depleted, since resin filters don't clog with contaminants the way carbon filters or micro-strainers do. The best way to detect depletion is to note that the unusually strong iodine taste is weak immediately after treating the water.

3) *Filtering.* Unlike boiling or chemical treatment, filtration literally cleans the water by straining out suspended solids, turning murky water clear. Filters also remove most but not all microorganisms. Some filters remove chemical impurities as well. Filters fall into two general types: gravity-fed, which relies on gravity to pull water slowly through the filter; and pump-fed, in which water is forced through the filter with a hand pump. The nice thing about pump models is that within the span of a few minutes you can stoop over a stream, fill your bottle, suck it dry, then fill it again before moving on.

A filter's basic task sounds simple: It removes organisms and particles. That's not easy, though, given the teensy-weensy size of the critters. It takes a very fine filter, a microstrainer, to catch them. Two types of filters are commonly used.

Membrane or surface filters: Thin sheets perforated with precisely sized holes let water pass easily through, while particles larger than these holes collect on the filter surface. These filters tend to clog quickly but are easy to clean and have a long service life.

Depth filters: Thick, porous materials such as compressed carbon or unglazed ceramic trap particles as water moves through a complex fibrous matrix instead of blocking particles larger than a given size at the filter's surface. Depth filters can be partially cleaned by backwashing (reversing the water flow) or by brushing the outer surface. Even with regular cleaning, depth filters will eventually clog and need to be replaced.

The size of a filter's pores determines which organisms it can remove from water. Pore sizes are measured in microns. Remember that a period is some 600 microns fat. It's unrealistic to measure all the openings in a filter element, so the most common way to determine effectiveness is to "challenge" it in a lab with water containing a known concentration of particles of a specific size and number. The result is a pore-size rating based on the size and amount of particles that can pass through the filter.

Pore-size ratings are commonly expressed as either "nominal" or "absolute." Since there is no standardized method for determining "nominal," the ratings have little value when you're comparing different filters. An absolute rating is just that—no particle larger than the rated size passed through the filter during testing. When filter shopping, use the absolute rating as a guide.

To reliably remove the most common backcountry cootie— Giardia cysts—a maximum pore size of four microns is recommended. Many filters have the required 0.2-micron pore size to remove bacteria as well. But because viruses can be as tiny as .0004 micron, so small they can be seen only with an electron microscope, no field device that relies solely on filtration can reliably remove them.

There's a difference between water filters and purifiers, which kill or remove bacteria, viruses, and protozoa. The only field device currently available that meets stringent Environmental Protection Agency purification standards is the PUR Explorer, which combines chemical treatment with filtration, using a resin-bound iodine element that acts as a contact disinfectant.

The First Need and MSR WaterWorks brands contain activated carbon filters. Besides removing microorganisms, these two carbon filters eliminate a range of organic chemicals such as pesticides, herbicides, and chlorine, although they won't remove dissolved minerals such as salt. This broad range of filtration is caused by the exceptionally porous structure of carbon and by "adsorption," the adhesion of molecules to a solid surface.

One key caveat regarding adsorption: There are limits to the quantity of chemicals or microorganisms a carbon filter can hold by this process. After the threshold for a particular material is reached, the filter no longer removes that substance from that water, and previously adsorbed material can be released. That's why manufacturers recommend replacing carbon filters periodically, regardless of whether they show signs of clogging.

Remember, to get the best performance out of your filter, clean it properly during regular use and before long-term storage. Follow the maker's instructions carefully.

One point needs to be stressed: Plan your water needs before you leave home. Consider the biological and chemical hazards you may encounter and match them with a suitable filter, disinfectant, or combination of the two. Think before you drink, because the consequences of getting sick in the backcountry range from annoying to life-threatening.

WATER LORE GUARANTEED TO MAKE YOU SICK

Myths surrounding water purification abound. Perhaps the best known is that water drawn from running streams is safe. Not so. In fact, guides in Minnesota's Boundary Waters Canoe Area Wilderness recommend drawing water from the centers of lakes or slow-moving rivers. Heavier-than-water Giardia cysts tend to sink to the bottom in quiet waters, while a fast-moving stream keeps them suspended.

Another myth is that freezing will purify. Truth is, most disease-causing bacteria are resistant to freezing. "Yellow snow" jokes aside, remember that clean snow is preferable to frozen surface water.

Then there's the old miner's belief that liquor will cleanse water. Although rubbing alcohol is a topical disinfectant, it should *never* be taken internally, and alcohol meant for drinking can't be relied on to sterilize water in the field.

PRESERVING PURITY: WHAT YOU CAN DO

What's the single most important technological contribution to human health and well-being?

Obviously, it's the flush toilet. Think about it. The lowly water closet vastly improved humankind's crude waste-removal practices, which had been putting parasites, bacteria, and viruses in the drinking water. The long-term result has been to raise the quality of life and extend its duration.

The problem is that the backcountry isn't equipped with toilets. It does have birds and trees and squatting spots with great views, though. (No one ever feels the need to take a newspaper to the woods.) Improper disposal of human fecal material can have a dramatic impact on the quality of the backcountry water supply. Here's what you should know to prevent water contamination.

• Dispose of feces or urine at least 200 feet from water. Use surface disposal of feces in low-use areas and cat holes where use is higher.
• If you use soap (try not to), make sure it's phosphate free. All dish washing should be done at least 200 feet from a water source. Don't concentrate wastewater in a single location; scatter it. In bear country, dispose of wastewater in a sump hole.
• Don't wash food particles off pans, dishes, or cooking utensils—wipe cooking implements clean. Pack garbage out.

THE INFAMOUS GIARDIA

Giardiasis probably has the dubious distinction of being the most talked about and most feared waterborne microorganism. It's commonly called "backpacker's fever" and "beaver fever," although the second tag is a bit unfair. Conventional wisdom long held that beavers spread Giardia cysts by untidily defecating in and near water. But studies show that beavers downstream from Forest Service campgrounds have a higher rate of Giardia infection than do those in true wilderness areas. The conclusion: Even more prolific and untidy animals (humans) share the blame.

The Giardia parasite takes on two different forms during its life cycle: the trophozoite, which lives and breeds in the intestine of the host (that's you), and the tough-walled cyst, which can survive for months in water. Once ingested, the cyst breaks down and releases up to four trophozoites. Once it has reached your intestines, a single trophozoite can produce up to one million baby parasites within 10 days.

Drinking as few as six of the microscopic cysts can cause infection. Six to 20 days after infection, diarrhea, abdominal cramps, fatigue, and vomiting may start. Some sufferers experience weight loss. The symptoms persist for 10 days to two weeks and can be treated with prescription drugs. The good news out of all this is that only 25 percent of those infected develop symptoms.

One other parasite deserves mention. *E. granulosus* is a tapeworm found in areas frequented by moose. It's infamous on Isle Royale National Park in Lake Superior, where the wolf and moose populations ensure plenty of homes for the tapeworm. Eggs are ingested and reproduce to form cysts in the lungs and liver. Boil and filter your water in moose country, although you're probably safe using a filter with an absolute pore size of 25 microns or smaller.

THE IMPORTANCE OF WATER

Losing and replacing water is a part of your body's daily routine. You lose about three quarts a day through breathing, perspiration, and waste removal. Strenuous backpacking, especially in high temperature, means additional water loss.

How do you know when to increase your water intake and by how much? The sensation of thirst doesn't accurately reflect your body's needs. You may have lost up to one percent of your body weight before the thirst signal kicks in, and the sensation of being thirsty may disappear before the lost water is replenished. The key to staying properly hydrated is to start drinking before you feel thirsty and keep drinking even after you feel satisfied.

Exact fluid needs vary from person to person. Age, physical condition, activity level, body size and degree of acclimatization all influence the amount of water you should drink each day. As a general rule, drink at least 16 ounces of water before hitting the trail, then replenish yourself with four to six ounces every 20 to 30 minutes. To fine-tune your water needs in the field, monitor the volume and color of your urine and frequency of urination. If you're producing clear urine at least five times a day, you're drinking enough. Cloudy or dark urine or urination less than five times a day means you should drink more.

chapter four:
HANDLING MEDICAL DILEMMAS

One item, your first-aid kit, should be the center around which you pack all the other gear. It's the most important item you hope you'll never have to use. When assembling (or buying) a first-aid kit, keep the following in mind.

• Check your first-aid kit before each trip. There are expiration dates on most medical supplies, so read the labels! Moisture, heat, and cold can also destroy the efficacy of first-aid items during a trip. Don't discover this in the boonies.

• Know how to use *everything* in your kit. Why carry a suture kit or a medication unless you understand its use? Besides, it could be dangerous for your partners if you try to administer unfamiliar medical treatments.

• Almost everything in your first-aid kit is designed to ease pain and speed healing of relatively simple medical problems. In a critical situation, it's your knowledge and how you use it that make the difference between life and death.

• The perfect first-aid kit is probably impossible to assemble, simply because if you spend enough time in the backcountry, sooner or later you'll wish for something you don't have. Kits reflect personal preferences as well. One small strip of moleskin might hide in your kit for years, while your companion might use a yard of the stuff every day. Think through carefully what you put in your first-aid kit.

• Off-the-shelf kits were once little more than a plastic box containing a few adhesive bandages and a tube of antiseptic cream. Now manufacturers are consulting wilderness-minded doctors who suggest items that would probably never cross your mind. These newfangled kits are better than the ones most non-M.D.'s could put together at home, and they're well worth the money.

THE ULTIMATE FIRST-AID KIT

Dr. William Forgey is arguably North America's most sought-after expert on wilderness medicine. Besides his medical training and wealth of firsthand wilderness experience, including more than 20 trips into the remote reaches of Canada's Northwest Territories, he is author of the classic book *Wilderness Medicine.* He wrote it for the everyday outdoorsperson, "people who were going to be out on their own for quite a while where rescue wasn't an option . . . people who had only the most rudimentary first-aid skills."

Drawing on his experience as an emergency-room physician and his practical understanding of what could and couldn't be done in the field, he set out to pen a usable, action-oriented book on the diagnosis and long-term care of illness and injury. The level of sophistication had to be adequate to provide care beyond the limits of first aid but simple and "unscary" enough that the layman would feel competent in doing it.

"That was a pretty big challenge," admitted Dr. Forgey, "but I was a physician, and I had been a layman recipient of these various problems, one who, frankly, abhorred a lot of medical manipulations anyway."

Dr. Forgey is quick to allay any misconceptions about the real risks of wilderness travel. "Most people, when they think about wilderness medical care, are thinking in terms of a big wound that needs suturing. 'How do I handle appendicitis out there?' is the other big question. But the most serious thing you could run into is hypothermia. The most common things you *will* run into are going to be friction blisters and maybe thermal burns, sprained ankles, and sometimes a knee injury." Parents should be particularly aware of hypothermia and earaches in children. "It sounds kind of mundane, but real wilderness emergencies are almost nonexistent."

That's why he feels each item in a medical kit should be given careful consideration. "There are a few things you can carry that will make things convenient; then there are more items you can carry that will make things more convenient. You reach a limit, though, where you're carrying too much."

Dr. Forgey considers one item essential. "Look at the most common problems that occur: sunburn, friction blisters, thermal burn. If I could afford almost nothing in weight or cost or bulk, I'd carry a Spenco Second Skin kit. It's just so usable for so many things. It's also nice to have something along for a bad headache or fever."

DOC FORGEY'S KIT

2 pkgs. Coverstrip closures, ¼ inch by 3 inches
1 Spenco Second Skin dressing kit
1 bulb irrigating syringe
5 pkgs. Nu-Gauze, high-absorbent, sterile, two-ply, 3 inches by 3 inches
1 Surgipad, sterile, 8 inches by 10 inches
2 rolls Elastomull, sterile roller gauze, 4 inches by 162 inches
10 Coverlet bandage strips, 1 inch by 3 inches
1 roll tape, hypoallergenic, ½ inch by 10 yards
1 1-oz. tube hydrocortisone cream, 0.5 percent (soothes allergic skin)
1 1-oz. tube triple-antibiotic ointment (prevents infection)
1 1-oz. tube Dibucaine ointment, 1 percent (local pain relief)
1 ½-oz. bottle tetrahydrozoline ophthalmic drops (eye irritation)
1 ½-oz. bottle Starr otic drops (ear pain, wax)
1 ½-oz. tube micronazole cream, 2 percent (fungal infection)
24 Actifed tablets (decongestant)
24 Mobigesic tablets (pain, fever, inflammation)
24 meclizine 25 mg tablets (nausea, motion-sickness prevention)
2 ammonia inhalants (stimulant)
24 Benadryl 25 mg capsules (antihistamine)
10 Bisacodyl, 5 mg (constipation)
25 Diasorb (diarrhea)
25 Dimacid (antacid)
2 pkgs. Q-tips, sterile, 2 per package
1 extractor kit (snakebite, bee sting, wound care)
6 1-oz. vials (for repackaging the above)
1 Over-pak container (to hold the above)

To obtain some of these medical-kit supplies, contact: Indiana Camp Supply, P.O. Box 211, 1001 Lillian St., Hobart, IN 46342; (219) 947-2525.

DON'T FORGET THE BUG REPELLENT

Everyone has horrible bug stories: swarms so thick they blacken the sky; insects so tenacious they chuckle when you smack them in midbite. In a perfect world, there would be no nasty bugs. In a perfect world, there would be the perfect insect repellent—one that lasts all day, isn't greasy, doesn't stink or dissolve plastic, doesn't burn your eyes, doesn't dry out your skin or give you a rash.

There are at least 40 repellents available, all different, all carrying the promise of a bite-free day in the woods. Which one to choose and why? The following answers to the most frequently asked questions about repellents may help you.

Why do mosquitoes bother me more than they bother my friends? If you're convinced mosquitoes single you out, you're probably not paranoid. When the female mosquito looks for food, she picks the best meal around—usually the person who gives off the strongest natural attractants. "If you're with some people who have stronger natural repellents than you, then you'll get bitten more," says Carl Schreck, a nationally known research entomologist with the U.S. Department of Agriculture.

Lactic acid (produced by muscle movement) and carbon dioxide (produced when you breathe) are believed to attract mosquitoes, but scientists are still looking for other attractants.

What is the best repellent? There's little disagreement that a colorless, oily, and slightly smelly liquid called DEET (short for N,N-diethyl-meta-toluamide) is the best. DEET comes in the guise of lotions, creams, sticks, pump sprays, and aerosols in strengths ranging from 5 to 95 percent. The list of insects that can't stand it includes mosquitoes, no-see-ums, fleas, ticks, gnats, and flies.

How much DEET is enough? If a little DEET is a good thing, then more must be better, or so goes the reasoning. But it's not wise logic, according to the results of a military test of three repellents conducted at Everglades National Park, Florida. During 20 hours of testing over four days, volunteers using the military's standard 75 percent DEET formula on their uncovered arms and heads were bitten an average of 29 times. The surprise was that the other repellents with half the DEET worked twice as well, suggesting that a long-lasting repellent with about 35 percent DEET provides at least as much protection as a stronger formula.

Any side effects from DEET? High concentrations feel unpleasantly oily and can melt plastic, watch crystals, and paint finishes. Although DEET is safe on nylon, cotton, and wool, it can damage rayon, acetate, and spandex. Test an inside seam of polyester/cotton blend clothing to see if DEET discolors or softens it. DEET can irritate eyes and sensitive skin and can dry skin. Allergic reactions have been reported. Using a low concentration may reduce irritation.

After applying DEET, wash your hands, or keep them away from your eyes and mouth. Never spray a repellent on your face. Instead, spray it on your hands, then rub your face.

Is it safe for children? Only in low concentrations and when used sparingly. DEET is quickly absorbed through the skin; 48 percent of an application is absorbed within six hours. The most common side effect is a rash, but in rare cases, irritability, anxiety, behavioral changes, abnormal movements, lethargy, and mental confusion have been reported. Repellents are, of course, poisons and can cause death if swallowed, so keep those bottles away from the kids.

Will it work against ticks? Clothing sprayed with an environmentally sound insecticide known as permethrin, plus a DEET repellent on the skin, is the best protection against ticks. Permethrin is sold as Permanone Tick Repellent aerosol in lawn-and-garden and sports stores. In military tests, 0.5 percent permethrin was sprayed on clothing, and the treatment was 100 percent effective against ticks. A 20 percent DEET spray was 86 percent effective.

Will my repellent stop wasps? No repellent is effective against bees, yellow jackets, and wasps, but using common sense helps. Leave your flowered-print shirts at home, along with sweet-scented lotions and perfumes. As far as the bee knows, a rose by any other name smells just like lunch. Yellow jackets and hornets also enjoy sharing your meal. Keep foods covered and garbage tightly wrapped, and don't try to wave off any invaders. It just makes them angry.

Are there other insect-repelling options? Mosquito coils are best known in Asia, Africa, and South America, where they are often used at night to ward off mosquitoes. The smoldering rodlike spirals release both smoke and insecticide. They can be particularly effective at clearing mosquitoes from the immediate area surrounding a campsite. The coils work best in still air and should not be used within a confined area such as a tent or cabin. The coils are sold through outdoors catalogs and in many Asian markets.

The Environmental Protection Agency has approved both the natural insecticide pyrethrum (from the pyrethrum flower) and a synthetic substitute, allethrin, for use in the coils. Only a few other countries, including Malaysia, Singapore, and Thailand, have set similar standards. Because DDT and lindane are cheap, these banned substances are used by some manufacturers. Hong Kong, which exports many goods to the United States, does not regulate the coils. "Not everything that comes into the country is checked," says Ronni Carey, a pesticide specialist at the National Pesticide Telecommunications Network in Lubbock, Texas. Read the label before buying mosquito coils.

An electronic unit sold through specialty catalogs emits a high-frequency sound that is supposed to repulse mosquitoes, gnats, sand flies, and black flies. The size of a cigarette lighter, it hooks onto your belt and is powered by a battery. The buzz is barely audible to humans and is claimed to keep insects six to eight feet away.

My skin is sensitive to DEET; what can I use? Eucalyptus oil, the original 6-12 (2-ethyl-1, 3-hexanediol), and the old standby citronella (an oil extract from a lemon-scented Eurasian grass) are sold in health-food stores and camping-goods stores. They're a good choice for children, although they must be reapplied frequently. Avon's Skin-So-Soft, a bath oil, is widely used as a repellent with differing reports on its effectiveness.

Can reading labels tell me how effective a repellent will be? The first indicator of a repellent's effectiveness is the amount of DEET it contains (about 35 percent seems best). Next, check to see if it's a long-lasting or controlled-release formula. Finally, compare the volume and type of application. Lotions provide the most even coverage. Repellent bottles and cans range from one ounce to six ounces, all with varying concentrations of DEET.

Is it possible to avoid bugs? You could stay home, but besides that, you can minimize your aggravation. Check with the local ranger for peak insect months. Some bugs, like mosquitoes, are out in force certain times of year. Pitch camp high, away from meadows, marshes, and running water. Go to bed early in a mosquito-proof tent; mosquitoes are most active at night.

BUG BITES

Step outside and you're in the world of the insects. Step into the backcountry and some insects will bite or sting you—it's that simple. But it helps to know how to minimize your contact with insects and how to treat their bites and stings.

Mosquitoes. Camp in open, breezy areas away from still water. Avoid dark-colored clothing. Wear clothing too thick for mosquitoes to penetrate. In warm weather, net underwear under light cotton clothing adds bulk but allows ventilation. Wear long-sleeved shirts and long pants. Use DEET.

Bees, hornets, wasps. Avoid scented soaps and lotions as well as brightly colored clothing. Insects are attracted to food, so keep a clean camp and don't leave food or beverages exposed. Check damp clothing and towels before using. Bees, hornets, and wasps nest anywhere that provides cover—in trees or logs, or even underground.

Fire ants. Watch for the distinctive foot-tall mounds. Waterborne fire ants will sting on contact.

Scorpions. Shake and knock boots together before putting them on. Shake out and inspect sleeping bags and clothing. Wear shoes in camp at night.

Blackflies, gnats. Camp away from running water. Use a well-ventilated tent with fine-mesh netting on windows, vents, and doors. Keep collars, sleeves, and cuffs tightly closed. Use DEET and be sure to apply it under clothing edges.

Ticks. Wear a hat, long-sleeved shirt, and long pants. Tuck pants' legs into socks. Apply repellents containing permethrin to your clothing. In prime tick habitat (tall grass or under-brush) keep to the center of the trail. Wear light-colored cloth-ing so you can see the dark-colored ticks.

IF YOU GET BIT

Bees, wasps, and fire ants. Wash the area with soap and water to reduce the possibility of infection. Apply a cool pack (a stream-dampened towel, for instance) for 20 minutes. Carry an oral antihistamine such as Benadryl in your first-aid kit to help control swelling and itching.

Mosquitoes, blackflies. Wash the bite and take an oral antihistamine to help reduce swelling and itching. A paste of baking soda and water will provide some relief from mosqui-to bites.

Scorpions. The vast majority are no more venomous than a wasp. Treat with a cold pack and take an oral antihistamine. The exception is *Centuroides sculptuatus,* a yellow or green-ish yellow scorpion about one-half to three inches long found in Texas, New Mexico, Arizona, Southern California, and northern Mexico. Immediate medical attention is vital.

Ticks. Grasp the skin with tweezers directly below where the tick is attached. Pull up, removing the tick and a small bit of skin. Wash the bite with soap and water.

COMMON WILDERNESS MEDICAL EMERGENCIES

During the frigid winter of 1811–12, thousands of Napoleon's Moscow-bound troops were dying from exposure to the elements. French Surgeon General Baron Larrey noted that those huddled closest to the roaring fires each night were the first to fall dead. In what's thought to be the earliest recorded field treatment for hypothermia, he made the nearly frozen soldiers sit back from the flames, thereby saving countless lives (probably because the rush of acid-rich, chilled blood from the extremities to the body's core was slowed until it could normalize before hitting the heart; this lethal phenomenon is known today as "after-drop").

The observant and ingenious Larrey also trained a crew of field medics to save time and lives by tending to the wounded before they were carried to his hospital. He became known as the father of prehospital medical care. Despite his medical discovery, it was not enough to help win the war. The Russians merely bundled up in heavy robes and let winter destroy the freezing French. Larrey's efforts did, however, form the basis of what would ultimately be known as wilderness medicine: the treatment of injuries or illnesses in a harsh environment far from definitive care.

These days there are a slew of Larrey wannabes running around in the woods. They work for a variety of organizations with acronyms like NOLS and SOLO, and like their Napoleonic predecessor, they teach wilderness medical techniques, deal with medical emergencies, and occasionally save a life. They were asked "What are the most common wilderness medical problems you encounter, and how do you treat and prevent them?" Here are their answers.

1) Tod Schimelpfenig, safety and training director, National Outdoor Leadership School (NOLS): "Over the past five years, 53 percent of our wilderness injuries have been sprains or strains. Our field instructors are taught to immediately RICE (rest, ice, compress, and elevate) sprained ankles. After 20 to 30 minutes of RICE, the ankle is allowed to rewarm naturally. Then we check the extent of the damage by letting the student walk on it. Recurrent ankle injuries might be prevented by wearing high-top boots or an air splint, taping, or simply emphasizing trail awareness.

"About 60 percent of our wilderness illnesses have been non-specific viral syndromes and diarrhea. Field treatment for diarrhea is limited to rest and plenty of fluids. Instructors carry some medications for diarrhea. We have seen a substantial reduction in the incidence of viral illnesses and diarrhea with improved hygiene and water-disinfection practices."

2) Dave Tauber, director of education, Stonehearth Open Learning Opportunities (SOLO): "Besides strains, sprains, and fractures, dehydration is common. Thirst is a poor indicator of dehydration, and the patient is usually well into a dehydrated state before feeling thirsty. Headache, fatigue, and loss of strength are better indicators. When you start making irrational decisions, you're seriously dehydrated. Untreated, it can be fatal. Drinking plenty of water is the proper treatment and the way to prevent the problem. Drink ahead of time. Make yourself drink on a schedule. Your urine should be clear, and there should be lots of it. I recommend plain water. If you prefer sport drinks, dilute them by at least 50 percent."

3) Keith Conover, M.D., Appalachian Rescue Conference: "Although they're usually considered non-emergencies, it's the little problems, especially blisters, that take up most of your time. The standard recommendation for blisters is to leave them intact, but that's not practical when you've got to put your boots on and keep hiking. My recommendation is to carefully clean the area thoroughly, then prick the blister with a needle, and gently press the fluid out. Something non-sticky, like reversed moleskin, should be placed over the drained blister before it's covered with a protective layer. Blisters can often be prevented by wearing two pairs of socks, keeping your feet dry, and applying moleskin to hot spots before they become blisters."

4) Melissa Gray, co-director, Wilderness Medicine Institute: "We did a survey several years ago and asked outdoor leaders about the medical problems they most often face. Their number-one answer was small superficial wounds, including blisters. To treat a small bleeding wound, let it bleed to a stop, which cleans the wound. If you don't have antiseptic, wash the wound with soap and clean water. You don't want to leave soap or even iodine in an open wound, so always finish by flushing with clean water. Cover the wound with a sterile dressing and check it daily for signs of infection."

5) Peter Both, M.D., president, Wilderness Medical Associates: "The most common problems backpackers face are what I call balance issues. We are challenged (by the environment) to maintain a thermal balance, a calorie balance, and a fluid balance. The cold challenge is answered by balancing heat loss and heat gain with appropriate clothing and activity levels. Energy needs are balanced by taking in the right amount of calories. You must drink enough water to keep your internal fluid level balanced."

DISPELLING MEDICAL MYTHS

Along with many common medical problems are common misconceptions that can seriously worsen an injury. Here are some of the most widely known medical myths that can lead to trouble.

Myth: Use a tourniquet to stop serious bleeding.

Truth: Serious bleeding can almost always be stopped without a tourniquet. Tourniquets violently crush blood vessels and other tissues, cutting off all blood flow. Everything beyond the tourniquet starts to die from lack of circulation. In the wilderness, small wounds are best left uncovered to stop bleeding on their own, since they self-clean in the process. For large wounds, grab a bandanna or shirt, cover the wound, and press down hard where the blood is coming out. Elevate the wound above the person's heart. Maintain direct pressure and elevation until the bleeding stops, then clean, dress, and bandage.

Myth: A shot of liquor will warm a hypothermic person.

Truth: Booze has the reverse effect. Alcohol causes blood vessels to dilate, giving a warm feeling but actually increasing heat loss through the skin. It also impairs judgment and interferes with coordination. Both effects can be deadly.

Myth: Rub snow on frostbite.

Truth: Hard, frozen body parts should be wrapped in dry, insulating material (a wool sweater, long johns, and so on) until the person can get to a hospital. Soft, pliable frozen parts should be rewarmed only with gentle, skin-to-skin contact. No fires or hot stoves or brisk rubbing! Once thawed, frostbitten extremities should be wrapped to prevent refreezing.

Myth: Put butter on burns.

Truth: Anything oily is bad for a burn. Initially, the oil traps heat and furthers the burning process. Later, the grease holds bacteria and dirt and makes it difficult to wash the wound. Instead, plunge the burn into cool water or wrap it in cotton cloth soaked with water. Keep up the cooling for several minutes, then cover the injury with a sterile-gauze dressing, which you should have in your first-aid kit.

Myth: Cut and suck a snakebite.

Truth: The techniques favored in old cowboy movies remove only small amounts of venom, while producing horrible wounds that can easily become infected. Tourniquets are also no-no's. Even if someone is bitten by a rattlesnake, the odds of it injecting enough venom to be fatal are very low. Keep the person calm, gently clean the wound, splint the bitten extremity, and get the victim to a hospital. If the person can walk, have them move slowly, and take breaks often. The same procedure goes for a bite from a coral snake.

Only one suction device is recommended for snakebites: the Extractor from Sawyer Products. If used within three minutes after the bite occurs, the vacuumlike syringe removes up to 30 percent of the venom.

Myth: Immediately soak a sprained ankle in warm water to speed healing.

Truth: Heat increases swelling and slows healing. Sprains like cold. Immediate RICE is the best treatment. "Ice" doesn't have to be frozen water. It can be cold water, snow, commercial break-and-apply cold packs (the smaller ones fit easily in a first-aid kit), or evaporation from a water-soaked cloth. Keep up the RICE for 20 to 30 minutes, then let the injured area rewarm before trying to use it. Ideally, RICE should be employed several times a day for a couple days. When the swelling is gone, heat can be used to promote healthy, healing circulation. If the swelling returns, go back to the cold.

Myth: Someone "struck dead" by lightning is ready for the undertaker.

Truth: Sometimes the victim dies, but more often the heart has stopped and the breathing mechanism has been short-circuited by the electrical blast. Victims of lightning strikes can usually be saved with cardiopulmonary resuscitation (CPR), which is too involved to go into here. It's one of the most valuable lifesaving techniques you can learn, whether your travels take you to the woods or the mall.

Myth: Since the brain dies after being deprived of oxygen for four to six minutes, someone underwater that long is beyond resuscitation.

Truth: The colder the water, the longer a person can survive. Cold reduces the brain's need for oxygen. Once again, the treatment is CPR. Don't be surprised if it doesn't seem to be working at first. It takes a while, so keep it up, then get the victim to a hospital.

Myth: Never let someone who has a head injury sleep.

Truth: This refers to someone who has a swelling brain from a sharp blow or a fall. If pressure on the brain increases to the point where the victim can't stay conscious, surgery is usually required to ease the pressure. In the wilderness, a person's best chance of recovery may be to sleep with as little disturbance as possible while a rapid evacuation is arranged.

Myth: Clear water tumbling over sun-washed rocks is naturally purified.

Truth: Moving water stirs up bacteria and disease-causing protozoa, increasing the chance they'll be swallowed by a thirsty hiker. If you can't disinfect your water, try to take it from a still spot.

Myth: God protects the ignorant.

Truth: Ignorance is no excuse.

chapter five:
HIKING
WITH THE FAMILY

Little limbs. Muscles just beginning to take shape. Young lungs. Stamina that at times seems unflagging. But is it? When you take a child into the backcountry, you can't help but wonder how much a youngster can and should physically withstand. At what age will he be ready to handle his own pack or paddle? More important, how should you pace your child so she'll grow to love the outdoors experience and not grow bored with it?

"The way you work with young children in any physical activity is to let them pace themselves," says Mary Ann Robertson, Ph.D., a motor development specialist at the University of Wisconsin–Madison. "If you watch children on a playground, you'll see this. They'll go pell-mell, pell-mell, and then they'll stop running. Then they'll pick up and go again."

Children aren't the steady plodders adults tend to be, so don't set high expectations for a day's hike. Before about the age of 6½ years, they have no notion of long-term goals, such as wanting to be at a specific campsite by sundown. Children's concerns are more immediate and can change within minutes, especially if the task is monotonous, boring, or uncomfortable.

"They'll stop doing whatever's displeasing or discomforting," notes Vern Seefeldt, Ph.D., director of the Youth Sports Institute at Michigan State University. "They become belligerent about continuing." Because of this, scientists don't really know the limits of muscular endurance, power, and strength in children younger than 4½ years.

Fortunately, you can readily determine your child's hiking capabilities by taking walks around the neighborhood. Martin Sklaire, M.D., associate clinical professor of pediatrics at Yale University of Medicine, points out that this is both a readiness test and preconditioning. If your youngster tires three doors down the block, he's not ready for the trail. Repeat the walks, gradually increasing the distance, and keep them fun. "Eventually he'll be ready," says Dr. Sklaire.

With older children, consider their current activity level. Do they walk to school or ride a bike? How far? Children, like adults, benefit from this kind of conditioning. Don't expect a child to start out at the high end or even necessarily at the low end of the range. Start small, give kids a chance to get in shape, but don't make it a chore. You want to keep it enjoyable, and you don't want to risk injuries.

Like adults, older children, adolescents, and teenagers can suffer overuse injuries if they do too much too soon. They can get all the various "itises," such as bursitis and tendinitis. They can even suffer stress fractures. The best cure is prevention by using slow, progressive increases in training. Parents of budding hikers should follow a rule of thumb that beginning runners abide by: Increase the distance by no more than 10 percent a week.

If injury should occur to your child's growing bones, cartilage, or joints, it's not a matter to be ignored. Generally, parents will know that an injury from a fall on the trail should be examined by a physician. But discomfort and swelling that occur after a long day's hiking should also be checked. Ignore a seemingly innocent injury and it might lead to incomplete healing, with possible chronic pain in a joint, or to diminished bone growth.

The adolescent or teenage years, when your youngster is growing so fast you can almost see it, is not a time the child will necessarily make quick progress in the number of miles traveled. Lyle J. Micheli, director of sports medicine at Boston's Children's Hospital, explains that when bones grow, "everything else has to sort of secondarily stretch out. During a growth spurt, kids can get tired. The same kid who left you behind on the trail two years before may now need to back off a little."

Along with pacing, another preventive measure is gentle stretching before striding off down the trail. Have your child lie on his back, then pull one leg toward his chest while keeping his head and back flat on the ground. Have him hold the position for a few seconds, then do the same with the other leg. This stretches the lower back, buttocks, and backs of the thighs.

Or have your young one sit Indian-style, his folded legs as flat on the ground as possible and the soles of his feet pressed together. Have him draw his heels as close to his body as possible and hold the position for several seconds, then repeat. This stretches the inner thigh and groin muscles.

Keep in mind that a child's sense of balance evolves up to the adolescent years. "As they get into more precarious kinds of hiking and climbing in their older years, their sense of balance is affected," says Dr. Robertson. "A youngster who has to turn sideways to work his way through a narrow passage will find that trickier than walking forward. And descending feels scarier than climbing up." Falls and mistakes are part of learning, but be ready to reach out a hand or offer encouragement in a hurry. You may have to give up the notion of going all the way to the top if going back down will be precarious.

For children of all ages, and even more so during the early years, remember the importance of positive reinforcement—what psychologists call validation. Your child is trying to please you and waiting to hear that he's doing just that. "I think if we know nothing else about the development of motor skills, we do know that success, as the child perceives it, is crucial," says Dr. Robertson. "If you're giving positive reinforcement to your child as he goes along, you just can't measure what that will do for your youngster."

MATCHING AGE TO ABILITY

Infant. For hiking, wait until about 5 months of age, when your baby can sit up, has more regular sleep patterns, and cries less. Use a safe, approved carrier that allows him to look around. In hot weather, make sure your child continues to drink water from a bottle between breast/bottle feedings.

Toddler, ages 2 to 4. Toddlers have just learned to walk, and their sense of balance is still developing. Select moderate terrain with easy footing. A toddler's attention span is short, so vary activities every 10 to 15 minutes for a 2-year-old and every half an hour for a 4-year-old. Test your child with walks around the neighborhood: a half-mile or less at 2 years; a mile, working toward two miles, for older toddlers. In heat, remind the child to drink water often; until puberty, children are more vulnerable to heat stress than adults.

Young child, ages 5 to 7. Stick to trails with easy footing. Have the child carry only a light pack until better balance is achieved (about age 6), then limit pack weight to 25 percent

of the child's body weight, assuming he's not overweight. Look for big changes between ages 6½ and 7½: improved motor skills, and an increased attention span—from about one hour (at 5 years) to a couple of hours (at 6½ years). At this stage, day trips are possible if you vary trail activities. Don't go farther than three or four miles.

Older child, ages 8 to 9. Work up to six- or seven-mile hikes, allowing a full day with an easy pace. From this age on, kids will push themselves more, so gradual conditioning is important to avoid overuse injuries. The older child can visualize the goal of a day's hike and get motivation from seeing the miles go by. Give the child a copy of trail literature with mileage and landmarks on it. A child's sense of balance will not be fully developed until the teen years, so be prepared to help if footing is tricky.

Young adolescent, ages 10 to 13. Work up to eight- to 10-mile hikes. Gradual conditioning is important. Have lots of water on hot days. If you are planning a canoe trip, your youngster will probably be able to paddle 45 minutes at a stretch.

Teenager, ages 14 to 18. Distances of eight to 12 miles are possible after conditioning, but during the teenage growth spurt, your child is vulnerable to overuse injuries. A teen may need to ease off and go shorter distances than he could a few years before. With puberty, the ability to sweat increases, so a teen's water needs on a hot day are similar to yours.

TENTING WITH TOTS

Your family dream trip hinges on finding the perfect home away from home—the tent—because let's face it, you just can't rough it *too* much with kids. You've got to include some of the basic comforts of home, like a cozy place to sleep.

The perfect dome away from home should be freestanding, feather-light, weather-tight, and roomy enough for the mythical nuclear family—Mom, Dad, 2.16 offspring, and Lassie. It should be bugproof, be tough as a rumpus room, and have easy in-out access. Most important, you shouldn't need a Ph.D. in mechanical engineering to pitch the thing or a second-home loan to afford it.

It wasn't that long ago that family tents came in army-style canvas duffel bags and weighed more than one of your teenagers. The ideal family backpacking tent has yet to be developed, but if the new generation of designs is any indication, tent makers are getting close. Here's what to look for when purchasing a tent.

Ease of setup (and takedown). Simplicity and quickness are a must at the end of what may have been a trying day.

Stability. If you plan to pitch the tent in the open, where it may be windy, stability is a crucial factor. Heavier, bigger tents do better in windy conditions, because stability is directly related to the number of poles, and larger tents need more poles.

Weatherproofing. Your tent's primary purpose is to protect you from the elements. No sense having a tent if a steady drip-drip-drip saturates sleeping bags and occupants.

Ventilation. When you have four bodies, eight stinky feet, and high condensation potential, you don't want stagnant air. In general, however, more ventilation means less warmth.

Durability. Any items likely to rip, snap, bend, or unravel will do just that after being subjected to kid abuse.

Roominess. Living space is all-important. Just imagine a rainy afternoon with all of you confined to your tent. Get the picture? Go as big as you can.

FAMILY ACTIVITIES FOR YOUNG AND OLD

A child is a natural explorer, filled with curiosity, enthusiasm, and an ability to experience the world without reservation or judgment. As an adult, your great challenge is to direct a child's energy without quashing it and to encourage exploration, adding what you can to deepen an experience and expand its meaning.

The "whats" of things—the names, facts, and figures—aren't nearly as important as the more visceral reality of perception and emotion. Your child is more interested in the texture and shape of a tree or the story of its struggle to grow than in knowing its name. A sensitive, direct experience with all of its embedded information serves far better than an explicit factual explanation that isn't fully understood.

If you watch your child's signals and respond to the circumstances, you'll be able to engage in activities that will be productive and fun. Try some of the following activities.

"Shapes of Nature." Cut a collection of circles, squares, triangles, and rectangles out of heavy paper or cardboard. Punch a hole near the edge of each, run a loop of string through each hole, and tie the shapes together. Encourage your child to match the shapes with large and small objects and natural features—rocks, trees, mountains. The child can hold the shapes up to match them with large objects, and smaller objects can be placed on top of the cutouts.

"Listen, Smell, Touch, Tell." Blindfold the child and lead him to a selection of objects that can be touched, smelled, and/or heard—trees, a stream, flowers, boulders. Give the child enough time at each location to fully explore the object. Encourage him to make use of all his senses. Give direct suggestions such as "Touch it with the tips of your fingers." Ask questions to spark curiosity and imagination: "How many different sounds do you hear?" "Does it smell sweet like honey or sour like garbage?" Lead the child back to the start and remove the blindfold. This game helps a child sharpen perceptive skills by forcing him to rely on senses other than sight and encourages understanding that the outdoors is a rich environment filled with a multitude of smells, sounds, and textures.

"Sames and Differents." Have your child collect or locate a selection of four to six different things of various sizes and shapes—trees, rocks, leaves, clouds, and mountains. Pick one item and examine it closely. Next, have the child find something outside of the group with similar qualities. A leaf and a feather are both long and have lines radiating from a middle spine. That's their "same," but what's different? Explore the objects with your child, helping him detect and describe the similarities and differences. Ask challenging questions. If more than one child is present, make it a contest by keeping a tally of the "sames" and "differents" each describes. Continue until you have found and discussed a match for each of the items the child selected. This game combines the fun and excitement of collecting with a sharpening of perceptive, cognitive, and verbal skills.

A variation of this game is to compare the parts of different animals. This is particularly useful when introducing a child to something new and strange, like aquatic insects. Have the child pick a part of a familiar animal—a fish or a dog—and then try to identify the comparable part on the animal in question. With creatures as alien in appearance as a dragonfly nymph, this can initially be difficult, and you might have to ask prompting questions: "A fish lives underwater just like this nymph. It breathes with gills that flap. What do you think the nymph breathes with?" This game helps a child recognize the common patterns of shapes and functions of living things and lessens the fear of odd or unusual animals by connecting them with familiar ones. It also helps engender an appreciation of natural things based on values other than simple outward appearances.

"Ups and Downs." The variations of this game are limited only by your child's imagination. It can be played in any natural setting, from the ocean shore to the deep forest. The object is to broaden your child's view of the outdoors by narrowing and focusing his perspective. It's important that you engage in these activities when the child is in a calm, quiet mood and ready to be still for 15 to 20 minutes.

"Looking Up" is played by having a child lie still and quiet, flat on his back, watching the world that passes above. This game is particularly effective beneath a heavy canopy of trees or in a field of tall grass.

"Looking Down" is the opposite. Have the child settle into a comfortable position on his stomach and watch what goes on in the world that passes beneath his feet. This game is particularly suited to watching tide pools and streams. For a younger child less likely to sit still for a long period, have him peer through a cardboard tube from a roll of paper towels or toilet paper. This "telescope" adds an active element to the game, while helping the child concentrate on the smaller elements that make up the whole.

"Trails and Walls." These two activities, suitable for almost any setting, respect the smaller side of nature. "Tiny Trails" is created by laying a four-foot section of string on an interesting outdoor surface that's rich and full of life—a forest floor, a bed of mussels, or a mossy rock, for example. Follow the path with a magnifying lens as it winds through a tiny world made big.

To play "Small Walls," tie the ends of the string together and have the child lay it down in any shape he desires, then have him explore the newly defined territory with the lens.

As the child examines the world that flanks the path of the string or is contained within its borders, he loses himself in a place where blades of grass grow big as trees and beetles plow through tangled jungles like fantastic modern dinosaurs.

"Flashlight Walks." The night is a magic time when familiar daytime landscapes assume a new and often mysterious identity. This activity can be exciting and reflective, depending on the mood and temperament of the child and the manner in which you conduct the walk.

Select a familiar area or a well-marked trail. Often, a child who is afraid of the dark will be outgoing at night in the company of an adult and other children. Let him carry a light because it provides a sense of control and will help lessen fears. Keep an eye and ear out for animals, especially where trees meet meadows or clearings. If an animal is detected, have the child hold the flashlight close to his face, pointing the light toward the animal. This way he may detect the glow of the animal's eyes reflecting the flashlight's beam.

"Find Your Tree." This encourages empathy and sharpens perceptual skills. Blindfold and lead the child to a tree. Introduce him to the tree and encourage him to explore it; hug it, touch it, listen to it, and smell it. Prompt him to thoroughly examine the tree, and spark his imagination with questions about the tree's history and life. Once he feels he knows the tree, lead him away and remove the blindfold. Now it's time to "find your friend!" If you'll be staying at one campground for a while, encourage him to check on the tree. "Is it different in the morning?" "Does the tree have any babies growing nearby?" "What other friends does the tree have? Squirrels? Birds?" If you will be returning to the same place later, either on your present trip or subsequent outings, let the child know that he will be able to visit his friend again, and don't forget to let him say good-bye before you go.

"Lights Out." A walk at night that ends with everyone sitting in the dark can be mysterious, adventurous, a little frightening—and most kids love it! This variation on the "Flashlight Walk" opens the nighttime world to children. With flashlights in hand, walk the child to a spot you visited earlier in the day. Discuss the night as you walk. Talk about how some animals are sleeping and others are just waking up. Describe the animals that make the sounds you hear, and talk about how the dark lets the plants rest and catch their breath after a day in the sun. In short, put the night in perspective. It's the same place you visited earlier, but now it's hidden by the dark and filled with different animals. When you arrive at your spot, turn the flashlights off and sit quietly. Ask your child to listen for sounds that are different from those he heard in the daylight. "Are the odors different here at night? Why do you think some animals come out at night?"

BRING ROVER ALONG

Your pooch has backpacking in its ancestry. In North America, the Plains Indians, so readily associated with galloping horses, once had only dogs to help carry their loads. Horses, a European introduction, weren't widespread among Native Americans until the early eighteenth century. An Indian's dog often wore a packsaddle and pulled a travois, a net platform hung between two poles and attached to a harness around the animal. Often those poles were the lodgepole frames of tepees in transit and could support loads up to 50 pounds. A Spanish explorer once reported seeing 500 loaded work dogs following one another in a train.

Your next backpacking trip might be a good time to remind your dog of his roots and lighten your load at the same time. Working dogs (malamutes, Samoyeds, huskies), sporting dogs (spaniels, retrievers, setters), and herding dogs (collies, shepherds) make excellent backpackers, though just about any strong, willing dog can be put to the task.

Where to go. Though wild dogs once freely roamed, now there are regulations regarding where you can take your dog.

National parks allow only "pack animals" to transport equipment, and dogs aren't included in the category. Furthermore, most national parks prohibit pets of any kind in the backcountry, allowing them only under close restraint in park campgrounds and public areas. The reasons are both pragmatic and philosophical. The primary charge of the national parks is preservation; parks are refuges for native animals and plants. Dogs represent a non-native, controllable element in the park picture and for that reason are prohibited.

The Forest Service has no blanket policy regarding pets on its trails. The forest supervisor at each national forest sets regulations. When preparing a trip with your dog, call first. Most national forests do stipulate that your pet must be kept under "physical restraint"—that is, leashed at all times.

Wilderness areas have no roads or campgrounds and allow no mechanical devices. Wilderness areas in the national forest system are governed by the same rules. When planning your trip, check in advance with the forest supervisor.

Bureau of Land Management has no pet restrictions except in rare instances like in habitat restoration areas or designated wilderness areas. "Restriction" in these instances usually means a leash.

State parks vary on the pet policy. Some don't allow pets, but most do with the requirement of a leash. Many state parks also require proof of rabies inoculation before entering the park. Call ahead.

On public lands the reasons for restriction are both social and ecological. Dogs often disturb other visitors, and unrestrained dogs on trails can spook or harass wildlife and livestock. Although dogs have acute senses, including a good sense of direction, a dog away from his familiar surroundings can become disoriented and lost if allowed to wander.

Before hitting the trail, be sure your dog is obedient and responds to voice commands. Overly aggressive dogs should be left at home, but many dogs will be subdued when harnessed with a moderately heavy pack. At night, seek out isolated campsites to reduce the chance of conflict. It's your responsibility if your dog creates problems. National park regulations state that a dog observed injuring or molesting humans, livestock, or wildlife can be destroyed. Unleashed pets can be impounded, and the owner has to bail them out.

Sharing the load. If your dog is still in the trip picture, it's time to think about sharing the load.

Dog packs have one chief purpose: They'll hold items you ordinarily couldn't fit in your pack. That allows for a lighter load so you can take a longer or faster trip. Often, a dog carries only his own food, but a fit dog should be able to carry up to a third of his weight—so take advantage of it.

Dog packs are harder to find than backpacks, but several manufacturers make them in a range of sizes. A specialty mountain shop is the best place to start if you're interested in purchasing or renting a set for your dog. The packs on the market are designed for dogs as light at 20 pounds, and capacities range from about 750 to 2,600 cubic inches per set. Prices range from $30 to $75 and up.

The most important consideration is that the pack fits your dog comfortably, keeping the weight stable and allowing for ventilation. The packs shouldn't ride too high or hang too low across the dog's back and should be positioned horizontal to the ground to help maintain even weight distribution.

As in single-compartment backpacks, everything falls to the bottom of a dog pack. Compression straps help distribute the weight and volume within the pack. Some models offer lash tabs and rings so you can add gear to the outside of the pack. Any buckle or ring against the dog's coat, however, is a potential source of irritation or chafing, so make sure that it is concealed or lined with material.

Your dog won't be concerned about the fate of his load, so choose a heavy-duty pack and plan what gear your dog will carry. Expect that whatever you entrust to your dog will be shaken, rolled on, submerged, muddied, and battered. Consider double-bagging any items that can be water-damaged, or carry them yourself. Loaded dogs are usually unaware they are carrying extra width and are likely to bump into trees, rocks, and the legs of two-footed backpackers.

The fact that a dog is (usually) a wilder animal than you doesn't mean he's in shape. Make sure he gets adequate exercise just as you would, with two or three weeks of conditioning prior to your trip. Take your dog along for walks or runs. Have him wear his pack and slowly add weight to it. Check that the pads of his feet are toughening up; dogs get blisters, too.

When packing, bring along first-aid items for your dog: tweezers, peroxide, antibiotic ointment, cotton swabs, scissors, and maybe a pair of small needle-nose pliers for removing embedded thorns or splinters. Dog nail clippers are worth carrying because canine toenails are not retractable, and a broken nail that goes untrimmed can be crippling.

In colder weather, dogs of certain breeds can accumulate little ice balls between their toes that become extremely painful and can cut the skin. A layer of petroleum jelly between the toes prevents this.

Just like their masters, dogs are susceptible to waterborne diseases like giardiasis. They show the same symptoms as humans—loss of appetite, diarrhea, stomach pain—but the symptoms generally aren't as acute. Trying to keep a thirsty canine from a cold stream or lake can be a futile task, and purifying drinking water for your dog is a tedious chore. You can try preventative measures, but if you are hiking in an area where you know that the Giardia parasite is a problem, have your dog checked when you get home.

The companionship of a dog on the trail can offer more than just another strong back. If you are poorly prepared, your dog can become a liability to you, the environment, and other hikers. But if you plan well for both of you, you'll have found an invaluable backpacking friend.

chapter six:
BACKPACKING
ABROAD

It sometimes happens while you're reading *National Geographic*. All those wild places—Borneo, Bolivia, Botswana, Mongolia, Madagascar, Malaysia, Greenland, New Guinea, the Galapagos Islands. Tropical jungles teeming with wildlife. Remote rain forests. Unknown mountains. They're out there, growling and howling and shaking the earth, and you're sitting in your living room, wishing and dreaming.

Why, when you already know how to travel, camp, hike, navigate, read clouds, and dress for all kinds of weather, are you on your couch instead of out and about in the African bush? Don't say money, because backpacking abroad is not impossibly expensive. For $500 to $1,500, you can buy a round-trip airplane ticket to almost anywhere in the world.

And don't blame the language barrier. If you know how to smile and wave, there is no such thing. Take the time to learn the "traveler's 10-word dictionary" (hello, good-bye, food, water, yes, no, sleep, help, please, and thank you) in the language of your destination and you'll likely be welcomed with open arms.

So what's stopping you?

Here's the easiest way to start: Sitting right where you are, think of the wildest, most unusual, unbelievable, fantastic, far-fetched, faraway place you've ever dreamed of going. Decide to go there.

Let's say you've picked Timbuktu. First, where is it? Only geography professors and game show writers seem to know.

Time for research, so hike down to your library, manila file folder in hand. Go to the reference section and pull out a world atlas, flip to the index in the back, and thumb to the pages listed beside the word. Aha! Mali. Where's Mali? West Africa. Haul the atlas over to the photocopy machine and you have the first important piece of paper for your file folder.

If you're going there, it would be wise to know something about the place. Look up every book and reference you can find on Timbuktu, Mali, West Africa. What's the weather like in June? What language is spoken? What is the local religion? You may find out that in June it rains so hard the streets are filled with a foot of mud and mosquitoes eat people alive, but in October the place is beautiful. You may find they speak French, in which case it's a one-evening task to master the French version of the traveler's 10-word dictionary.

If, after a bit of homework, Timbuktu still fires your fancy, you'll need a few months to get ready. First, call the State Department and find out if there's a war quietly raging that hasn't been getting much press in your local newspaper. Bear in mind that the State Department tends to be ultracautious with its travel advisories.

Next, you'll need a passport. Can't leave home without it. Hike down to the county courthouse and pick up a U.S. passport application from the clerk of court. To get a passport you'll need proof of U.S. citizenship (birth certificate), proof of identity (driver's license), two photographs (identical two-inch by two-inch mugs get at least 12 extras for visas), and about $42. It usually takes about four weeks to get your pretty blue, eagle-embossed United States of America passport.

In the meantime, check into a visa and immunizations. This information should be in a travel book. Most European countries no longer require a visa, but many Third World countries do. Mali is no exception. Back to the library. Find the *Statesman's Yearbook*. It lists addresses and telephone numbers for all foreign embassies in America. Photocopy not only the information on Mali but the countries surrounding it as well. Call or write for visa information and applications.

Before leaving the library, go to the map room. Contrary to what you may think, most countries do have detailed topo maps. Find *World Mapping Today* (Buttersworth Publishers, London). It contains a listing of the map distributors for almost every square inch of the earth. Look up Mali. Photocopy.

If this book isn't available, look for an October issue of *Geotimes: A Publication of the American Geological Institute*. Every fall they publish a directory of all geoscience organizations (aka mapmakers). Photocopy.

One of the best map services in America is MapLink (25 E. Mason, Santa Barbara, CA 93101). Two of the best European map services are the German *Geo Katalog* (Internationalesz Landkartenhaus Gmbh, Postfach 80 08 30, D-7000, Stuttgart 80, Germany) and the French *Institut Geographique National* (136 bis rue de Grenelle, 75700 Paris, France). Write to whomever makes the large-scale topos, specifying exactly what you need (include reference numbers). Expect to pay $8 to $20 per map.

While waiting for your maps, call the federal Centers for Disease Control and Prevention (CDC) in Atlanta, Georgia, and ask them for a list of mandatory and recommended vaccinations for your destination. Also ask for a list of recommended prescription drugs for local diseases. Then call your local public health service and schedule the shots, which must be recorded in an International Certificate of Vaccinations. Get all of them! Being sick in a foreign country, especially in the outback of a foreign country, is no holiday. Many of these shots cannot be taken simultaneously, so you may need about a month.

Starting with the CDC list of recommended prescription drugs, read up on what diseases you are likely to encounter, then make an appointment with your doctor. You'll need a small, but powerful, medicine kit. For instance, if you are traveling to Timbuktu, your kit should have drugs to treat malaria, schistosomiasis, onchocerciasis (river blindness), giardiasis, tumba larva, and trypanosomiasis (sleeping sickness). You'll also want Lomotil (for loose bowels), mosquito repellent, petroleum jelly (for cracked feet), and antiseptic ointment.

Many diseases can be prevented simply by peeling all fruits and vegetables and purifying your water. Bad water is a big threat, and there are three common nasties that'll get you: parasites, such as Giardia; bacteria, which cause cholera, salmonella, typhoid, and a host of other illnesses; and viruses that can result in yellow fever, influenza, herpes, polio, and other more uncommon conditions. Most good water filters will strain out parasites and bacteria, but none stop viruses. The tried-and-true, lightweight iodine method is still the best (see chapter 3.)

Most airlines have toll-free numbers, so get on the horn, find the best deal, and make reservations. Start filling out the visa applications. Most will require you to submit not only your passport but your International Certificate of Vaccinations, two or three of those handsome mug shots, and proof of finances (a photocopy of your ticket to prove you can get out of the country). Mail them off and wait another two to four weeks for the visas.

Time for the final step: equipment checklist. For Timbuktu, your clothing should be light-colored and made of cotton. You should also take warmer clothing and raingear (Gore-Tex is the most comfortable); sleeping bag and pad; sunglasses, hat, and sunscreen; a money belt; a solar calculator for exchanging money (carry half traveler's checks, half U.S. $20 bills because greenbacks talk when nothing else will); solid, comfortable footwear; camera and journal; a two-liter water bottle. Stuff it all in a rugged, no-frills, comfortable backpack.

Recommended reading. The best shoestring travel guides are by Lonely Planet (Embarcadero West, 112 Linden St., Oakland, CA 94607; 800-229-0122). The series, which covers many of the world's major mountain ranges, is exceptional.

Sierra Club *Adventure Travel Guides* (Sierra Club Books, 730 Polk St., San Francisco, CA 94109; 415-923-5500) are another valuable resource.

If you're going for mountains, the *Climber's and Hiker's Guide to the World's Mountains* (Kelsey Publishing, 456 E. 100 North, Provo, UT 84606; 801-374-1747) is encyclopedic and has good detail maps.

The best standard atlas is *The Times Atlas of the World, Seventh Comprehensive Edition* (Random House, Times Books, 210 E. 50th St., New York, NY 10022; 800-733-3000).

chapter seven:
HIKING
IN HOT WEATHER

Your brain and body are critically interested in maintaining a comfort range of 97° F to 100° F, which averages out to 98.6° F. Put on a backpack, throw in a 90° F or 100° F day, add humidity, and you've got a potential conflict: dehydration, heat exhaustion, even heatstroke. When things get too warm inside, your brain's thermostat, the hypothalamus, triggers a process that dilates the blood vessels near your skin. Your skin warms through increased blood flow, and air circulation pulls the heat away from your body. The air also evaporates the sweat on your warm skin, which cools the blood as it returns to your body's core, including the brain, keeping everything within a healthy temperature range.

This human cooling system works fine if you encourage the process. In fact, all heat illnesses are preventable if you know how to keep a hot, humid day from turning against you. Here are a few suggestions:

• Allow yourself time to acclimatize. Early in the hot season or early into a trip to a hotter climate than you're used to, go easy for the week or two it takes your body to adjust to hotter temperatures. You can't handle the heat overload right away.

If you do push it too soon, you may experience painful heat cramps, which usually affect the legs and abdomen. Excessive sweating depletes salt stores, and pain results from muscle overuse. Though the discomfort may be great, the problem isn't serious. Merely stop and rest. Stretch and rub the hurting muscles. Drink water that has been lightly salted (¼ to ½ teaspoon per liter). If salt isn't available, munch salty snacks. When you feel rested and relaxed, resume your hike.

If the pain returns, take the rest of the day off, since overusing a salt-depleted muscle can result in permanent injury.

- Don't take salt tablets to prevent heat cramps. Your body needs to get rid of excess salts, so it flushes them out with valuable water, increasing the rate at which you dehydrate. "Salt tablets are five to 10 times stronger than necessary and should never be taken with less than one liter of water per tablet," says Corey Slovis, M.D., an emergency-room physician in Atlanta, Georgia, where heat illnesses are common.
- Avoid alcohol. It blunts the function of your hypothalamus, tricking your brain into thinking it's better off than it really is. Alcohol increases your dehydration rate and makes blood vessels dilate, so when your rate of evaporation slows, you absorb heat from the environment faster.
- Avoid antihistamines. Some of the stronger medications block your sympathetic nerves, which stimulate sweating. No sweat means no evaporation and no cooling.
- Shed a few pounds. Body fat reduces your ability to shed excess warmth. People who do well in extremes of heat tend to be long, lean heat dissipaters, while cold-weather enthusiasts are more often well-insulated heat retainers.
- Wear loose-fitting clothing, which lets air and moisture flow in and out and over your hot body. Wear a hat, especially one with a wide brim, to shade your heat-sensitive brain.
- Your body loses about three quarts of water a day through breathing, perspiration, and waste removal. Strenuous hiking in hot weather can increase the rate of water loss to as much as three quarts an hour. Be sure to drink plenty of water during periods of physical stress to prevent dehydration. "It's a matter of hydrodynamics," says Jean Storlie, a nutrition and fitness expert with Rush–St. Luke's–Presbyterian Medical Center in Chicago. "Your heart is a pump that circulates fluid through a contained system. When you don't have enough water in your system, your blood thickens, and it takes more pressure to push it through the vessels." Thicker blood doesn't carry carbohydrates, vitamins, and other nutrients throughout your body as effectively, so your energy level drops, and you start to feel dizzy, weak, and lethargic as you become dehydrated.
- Profuse sweating and loss of fluids can lead to a more severe, shocklike condition known as heat exhaustion. Fatigue, headache, nausea, vomiting, pale and sweaty skin, and a rapid heart rate are all symptoms. Your body-core tem-

Sun's angle, noon, Dec. 22

Sun's angle, noon, June 22

S

N

NORTH FACE

SOUTH FACE

As summer solstice approaches, days get longer and hotter, and shade gets harder to find.

perature may rise to 104° F, and you may feel light-headed. You might feel like a flu bug has attacked. Treatment is simple: Rest, preferably in a cool, shady place. Drink a minimum of one to two quarts of water to replace lost fluids. Cool water is best because it will be utilized more readily by your overheated body. Add salt to the water, but no more than a teaspoon per liter. Remove or loosen clothing, sprinkle water on your skin, and fan yourself to increase the evaporation rate.

• Slow down during the hottest part of the day, say around 2 P.M. Savvy desert dwellers conserve their strength and moisture by taking a midday siesta, then resume their labors when the heat is less intense.

• Rest. It's a simple-sounding suggestion, but it's vitally important when heat and humidity are high. Prop your feet up, and take it easy.

• If your core temperature reaches 105° F, you will move to a more dangerous stage and suffer heatstroke. Left untreated, you have an excellent chance of dying. If you were elderly and the problem had come on over a period of three to five days, leaving you sweatless and comatose, you would likely be the victim of classic heatstroke. Your problem, however, is exertional heatstroke caused by a high level of physical stress and dehydration. You are probably wet with sweat, red, and hot to the touch. Delirium, combativeness, and difficulty staying conscious are other telltale signs. Your overtaxed heart may reach 240 beats per minute. The decrease in oxygen to your brain may cause a seizure. Soon your liver will fry, your brain will boil, and you'll die.

"A fine line separates heat exhaustion from heatstroke," says Dr. Murray Hamlet, director of the U.S. Army Research Institute of Environmental Medicine in Natick, Massachusetts. Although exertional heatstroke is more common in fit, acclimatized folks who push themselves too far with too little water, it can happen to anyone. At about 106° F, the human body loses the ability to control its own temperature. From there, the victim's temperature may skyrocket, and saving his life will mean cooling him as quickly as possible. Do not give him anything to drink unless he is awake and coherent. Liquids do little to lower temperature, and the risk of choking is high.

Get him out of the sunlight and remove his clothing. Wet him down and fan him vigorously. Use cool or tepid water, not alcohol. If cold packs are available, place them in the armpits and groin and behind the victim's neck. If a cold mountain stream runs nearby, place him in it, keeping his head above water. A heatstroke sufferer has an increased body temperature, not a fever. Do not give him fever-reducing medications. After he has cooled, recheck him at least every half an hour for the next three to four hours. It is not uncommon for the temperature to rise again. Evacuation to a medical facility is recommended.

Preventing heat illnesses is an act of discipline. Drink before you feel thirsty and keep drinking after you feel satisfied. To fine-tune your water needs, monitor the volume and color of your urine and your frequency of urination. If you're producing clear urine at least five times a day, you're drinking enough. Cloudy or dark urine or urination less than five times a day means you should drink more.

"You can't overhydrate," says Dr. Hamlet. A liter of water every hour is reasonable in extreme conditions, or half that on a typical hot, humid day.

DESERT HIKING

Contrary to what you might think, a desert is not a vast wasteland, devoid of life and scenery other than bleached bones. Deserts are unique and beautiful ecosystems well worth a backpacking trip. There are certain considerations, however. For instance, timing. If you're planning an August trek through the Sonoran Desert, where the only shade is saguaro cactus and the wings of big buzzards, you'd be wise to bring a large umbrella, a camel train, and 100 goatskins of water.

The desert in spring, however, is a time of cactus flowers, pleasant temperatures, and hordes of winter-whitened visitors. Autumn offers cooling temperatures and rapidly declining crowds. Winter, the season when the desert seems undiscovered, when you can wear a T-shirt and easily find water, when the silence is deafening and the nights frosty—that's the best time of all!

The principle of timing is a daily as well as seasonal concern. In summer, the desert sun might rise by 5:30 A.M. and set as late as 9:30 P.M. Temperatures begin to max out about three to four hours after sunrise, so it's worth pacing yourself. The best rhythm for warm-season desert travel is to hit the trail early, travel until the day heats up, take a siesta in a shady location until the mercury drops, then take off again through the cool of evening.

Traveling in those magical hours Emily Dickinson called "the far theatricals of day," you'll be in good company. At sunrise and sunset, the kit foxes wander, the datura unroll their snow-white trumpets, and bats flit in silhouette across fiery pink skies. On well-delineated trails, with a full moon or a reliable headlamp, you can even experience the uniqueness of night travel.

Don't underestimate the sun, though. Before taking that first step each morning, paste your face, neck, and ears with a waterproof industrial-strength sunblock. Ultraviolet filtration sunglasses and a broad-brimmed hat are mandatory. The Foreign Legion–look cap with a neckerchief cape is popular.

Carry two sets of clothes. For daytime, light-colored cotton apparel is *de rigeur*. Simple mistakes, like packing only a black T-shirt, can kill you. Hospital scrubs are popular, but the open necks can lead to sunburn as can shorts if you forget the sunblock on your legs. After sundown, you'll need warm clothes because in all seasons but summer, desert nights are chilly.

In desert conditions, a gallon of water a day per person is the minimum. If you're counting on finding water, make certain your information is reliable and current because desert water sources are transient by nature. The three-gallon depression you drank from yesterday will probably be gone when you pass it on your way back. Giardia is a threat in the desert, but be careful with water filters because they plug up quickly in silty desert streams (see chapter 3). Often, even after treatment, desert water tastes like dishwater, so pour in drink mix and keep chugging. Staying hydrated is your first priority.

It's better to carry your own water in one- and two-liter bottles. If you put all your fluid in a single large jug and it leaks, you've got a full-blown catastrophe on your hands. Besides, your load will carry better with the smaller bottles. The weight of water—nine pounds per gallon with bottles— sounds like a logistical nightmare, but it isn't as bad as it sounds, since you'll carry less gear in warm weather.

Take food, for instance. On a cold-weather trip, your pack is stuffed with tons of food, a stove, fuel bottles, and lots of clothing. But appetites usually drop in the heat, so keep things simple. Have a cold breakfast and skip the stove. Forget the cook kit and eat finger foods.

A final note: Many desert trips offer the singular opportunity to become lost before reaching the trailhead. Long, unmarked access roads are standard. Signs are rare. For that matter, trails are rare, and maps are often outdated. Desert canyons are incised down into flat plains, and everything looks like table-top hiking until your route is unexpectedly cut off by a sheer precipice. That's what makes desert backpacking invariably challenging, fascinating, and fun. And believe it or not, it's safe if you follow the rules. Always remember, though, that you can't bend or break those rules.

chapter eight:
HIKING
IN COLD WEATHER

Contrary to popular opinion, winter camping is not the sole domain of mountaineers and masochists. Anyone who has backpacked in summer can, with a few adjustments in style and gear, make the transition from warm to cold. And to many, it's worth it. Camped out during the long nights of January and February, while your friends huddle around the boob tube or sip overpriced schnapps at the lodge, you can witness backcountry magic in the making. Your steaming dinner slides down better than any restaurant meal. As the temperature drops, the sap freezes, and trees crack like rifle shots. The aurora borealis, better known as the northern lights, ripples and shimmers like neon waves in the satin-ocean sky. The coyote's howl and the hoots of a great horned owl ring clearer through the crisp, cold air.

Even at 0° F, the cold is not as brutal as you think. To the contrary, you lie snuggled in your sleeping bag, warm and cozy, invigorated and excited. Winter camping is intoxicating when it gets into your blood.

Assuming you already know the basics of warm-weather backpacking and have rudimentary ability on cross-country skis or snowshoes, winter camping requires only a few different considerations and techniques.

First, if you have friends already involved in winter camping, ask if you can accompany them on their next short trip. Chances are they'll agree, since winter campers are always looking for partners. Don't be passive on these trips. Offer to help with all the chores so you can get experience in tasks such as cooking and pitching the tent, which require different approaches in winter. There is no better way to learn.

You can accelerate your education by participating in a winter camping course offered by an outdoor club or adventure travel outfitter in your area. Good instructional programs are designed to quickly transform beginners into experienced winter travelers. Still, nothing teaches more effectively than hands-on experience. If you have to get started on your own, progress gradually. A 15-mile trek isn't necessary to have a fine backcountry experience. At first, take a short trip afield with only a daypack loaded with essentials, then practice winter camping techniques in areas you already know or in your backyard if you live in snow country. Covered with a blanket of snow, parks and forests you thought were tame in July take on a distinct wilderness aura in January. Only when you feel at ease camping in the snow should you attempt an overnight backpack farther from civilization. The cardinal rule of winter camping is not to exceed your limitations. Here are some basic snow-camping tips.

Living and moving on snow and ice. Travel in winter takes longer, and days are shorter. Tasks that are usually easy, such as pitching a tent or obtaining drinking water, become more complicated. Learn to operate all your equipment while wearing gloves or mittens.

Finding a route. Deep snow frequently obscures trails, and rime ice often plasters trail blazes or markers. Proficiency in compass use and map reading is essential.

Judging weather. One day may be mild and drizzly, while the next can usher in subzero temperatures. Part of being weather-wise is knowing when it's safe to continue and when you should turn back.

Training. Physical conditioning is more important in winter backpacking than in summer, since loads will be heavier and trudging through snow is laborious. Being physically fit will let you have more fun and expand your possibilities. Carry high-energy foods on the trail, and drink before you're thirsty; a good rule of thumb is to take a few gulps at every rest stop.

Gear. Equipment costs to get started in winter camping are relatively low. Most of your regular summer backpacking gear will cross over, and the specialized gear you need can be rented, made, or purchased at end-of-year sales.

If snow depths rule out hiking, the most important consideration is whether to use snowshoes or cross-country skis. Snowshoes are superb on steep trails with lots of ups and downs or routes through heavy forests, and you can learn how to walk on them almost immediately. Skis are excellent on flat or gently rolling terrain that's free of underbrush but can prove difficult for newcomers to master. Many winter campers eventually end up owning both and decide which to use depending on the destination.

Other essential items of equipment you'll need include:

Socks and boots. Cold feet can be more than just a hindrance; they can lead to frostbite. You need boots that will fit over at least one pair of medium wool socks and another pair of heavy socks, while allowing room for toes to wiggle. The warmest sock combination is a neoprene sock under a vapor barrier liner (VBL) with a wool sock on the outside. The VBLs help prevent blisters by reducing the friction of the heel inside the boot and help keep boot interiors dry. Before you don socks and liners, try covering your heels in duct tape; the slippery outer surface reduces blister-causing friction.

The best footwear for snowshoeing is the leather-top, rubber-bottom pac boot with removable wool liner. Take along a spare pair of liners and alternate use. Cross-country skiers can get by with ankle-high, leather touring boots, since the constant motion while skiing keeps your feet warm. For campwear, down or synthetic-fill booties with nylon mukluks or overboots are great when the sun goes down. Seal your boots at least once a season. Store them on shoe trees, especially when they're wet, because it keeps them from shrinking. Rubber-banded, over-the-boot, insulated gaiters protect your boot leather and are more viable than double-boots.

Clothing. Snow camping requires clothing that will keep you comfortable from about -30° F to 40° F. A good ensemble should include wool or pile pants (*never* cotton!), two sets of polypropylene long johns, and wind pants. For above the waist, start with polypropylene long-sleeved underwear, a wool or pile sweater, a down jacket with hood, and a shell parka with hood. Add wool or polypropylene glove liners, wool or pile mittens, shell overmitts, a wool ski cap with ear flaps, a balaclava, and gaiters. That's your basic winter outfit. Keep all your clothing loose fitting for plenty of ventilation. If you overheat and sweat profusely, you set the stage for a long, cold, clammy night.

Sleeping bag. Choose down if you can afford it; otherwise, use a quality synthetic. To extend the range of your sleeping bag, use an extra-thick foam sleeping pad, a light liner bag or overbag, and possibly a nylon VBL.

Stove. Since getting water in winter almost always involves hours of melting snow, and because hot food is so important, take a reliable camp stove you know how to operate. Some models function better in the cold than others, but in general the white-gas stove you use in summer works fine in winter. Don't operate your stove inside your tent because carbon monoxide can build up, and there's always the chance of fire.

Pack. Back-hugging internal frame packs are generally more conducive to cross-country skiing than external frame packs. For snowshoeing, many people prefer rigid frames. Use whatever pack you have, but make sure it's roomy enough to hold all that extra gear.

Miscellaneous. A headlamp or flashlight with extra bulbs and batteries, roomy tent, small snow shovel, thermometer, foam seating pad, eating utensils, sunglasses or goggles, sunscreen, water purifier, water-bottle insulator, toilet paper, toothbrush and paste, first-aid kit, repair kit (for ski poles, stove, tent, etc.), candle lantern, and good paperback book.

THE DOWNSIDE OF WINTER CAMPING

When the mercury drops, there are several cold-weather health concerns to watch for.

Hypothermia. The number-one cause of death in the outdoors develops when the body's heat production can't keep up with heat lost. This sounds straightforward enough, but there's more to hypothermia than just getting cold. For one thing, the condition doesn't just chill the body; it also numbs the mind, impairing the ability to recognize that a problem exists. Even the most experienced outdoorsman can suddenly find himself lacking the sense to come in out of the rain.

Worse yet, hundreds die from hypothermia because of a major misconception: that it's strictly a dead-of-winter condition. People enjoying the great outdoors have been surprised by a brisk autumn breeze and have "frozen to death" with the thermometer hovering at 50° F. Boaters tossed into 70° F water have died. At seemingly harmless temperatures the process can take hours, so you may not realize what's happening. That's why hypothermia could be considered the trickster fox of outdoor illnesses.

Metabolically speaking, you're a fine-tuned machine that functions best when you're 98.6° F within. A drop of even a few degrees in your internal or "core" temperature and your body shifts gears. Blood flow to your extremities decreases. You feel cold. Your muscles try to generate heat, which causes you to shiver.

So far, so good. But these normal defenses are easily overrun by external conditions, like a sudden rainstorm or a freshening breeze, or by internal ones—lack of food or heat loss while resting, for example. Your core temperature drops, and moderate hypothermia sets in. Shivering becomes uncontrollable, and you might shuffle or stumble. You may slur your words, since control of finer muscles goes first, and you may act confused. Your brain is getting chilled, and if unchecked, your condition will worsen. Severe hypothermia sets in as your core temperature approaches the range between 90° F and 95° F. Some victims suffer amnesia, others feel strangely warm and strip clothing. Collapse, coma, and death by heart failure follow.

But hypothermia is so easily prevented, no one should die from it. Keep the machine running smoothly with high-energy foods (complex carbohydrates, proteins, and fats) and plenty of water (at least five quarts a day). Put on layers of clothing *before* you get cold or wet, since wet clothes accelerate heat loss five-fold and cold-water immersion can speed it by up to 25 times normal. If your feet are cold, simply put on a hat because up to 50 percent of your body's heat loss is from your head.

If the condition is mild, normal body temperature should return quickly. Try to slowly consume warm foods or liquids. After a while, try mild exercise—something simple, like stepping on and off a rock or log—to build body heat. If you're treating someone, make sure they don't wander off.

Moderate to severe hypothermia is a more complex problem. Treatment is critical but hardly follows common sense. If outside rescue is possible, end the exposure with shelter or dry clothes, and do nothing. That's right, do *not* try to rewarm the victim. Don't walk him around, and don't rub his hands and feet. Chances are, best intentions notwithstanding, you'll kill him. The reason is the after-drop. By now, the blood pooled in the extremities is well chilled. It has also turned acidic. Promoting circulation causes that blood to flow back to the body core, further chilling the heart and subjecting it to an acid bath few can survive.

That's not all. A cold heart is a sensitive heart. Jostling and pulling someone can trigger fibrillation. Instead of pumping, the heart quivers ineffectively. Gentle handling, such as cutting away instead of pulling off wet clothes, is crucial. Furthermore, when a body is deeply hypothermic, it's in what's known as a metabolic icebox. Breathing, pulse, and heartbeat have slowed so much they may appear absent. The victim seems dead. But a person can survive in this state for hours without permanent damage. History is full of seemingly frozen people who were assumed dead, only to recover upon rewarming. Hence, the somewhat morbid maxim "No one's dead until warm and dead." If evacuation isn't possible or is likely to take more than four to six hours, treatment must be initiated carefully. Rewarm the body core, not the extremities.

But the simple fact remains: Despite the best efforts, severe hypothermia is not effectively treatable in the field, and the best defense is prevention. Common sense and good intentions are fine but are no substitute for an informed approach and good judgment.

Frostbite. Nat King Cole was a great singer, but anyone who could rhapsodize about "Jack Frost nipping at your nose" would not make a good tent mate on a cold winter day. The problem is that sometimes Jack bites. When he bites hard, you can lose fingers and toes, even hands or feet.

When exposed flesh freezes, skin becomes white and firm to the touch. But hands and feet covered by clothing also get frostbitten, often severely, because the freezing goes unnoticed. The fact is, toes are the most common site for frostbite.

Exposure is not the only culprit; impaired circulation is often an accomplice. When blood vessels constrict, as they automatically do to conserve heat in the body core, extremities are robbed of adequate blood. Extremities, from your cold body's perspective, are big portions of you, like arms and legs. Tight-fitting clothes and shoes aggravate the assault. Your skin turns white and waxy looking, becoming painful just before it goes numb; then, without the warning bell of pain, freezing in the numbed skin extends to deeper levels. Ice crystals form between the cells, and your flesh becomes as hard as a piece of freezer meat.

Tragically, the severity of frostbite is difficult to judge until after your flesh thaws. Mild cases leave your skin red for a few days. Deep frostbite causes huge, fluid-filled blisters that can engulf your entire hand or foot. If the fluid is clear, the underlying flesh will probably recover, but blood-filled blisters signal dead tissue. Your flesh will turn black and eventually separate spontaneously; in other words, your fingers and toes will simply fall off. The discomfort of thawed, frostbitten flesh starts at "painful" and later goes off the scale somewhere around "excruciating."

When treating frostbite, it's as important to remember the *don'ts* as well as the *do's*. Don't rub the affected area. With ice crystals crowding against fragile cell walls, you might as well rub your body with ground glass. And don't thaw tissue unless you're absolutely sure it won't refreeze. A second freezing is far more damaging.

Mild frostbite can be treated by pressing a warm body part against the frozen area until feeling and color return. Placing a partner's frostbitten feet against your bare stomach is an excellent idea (and a sure sign of genuine friendship).

For severe cases, experts recommend immersion of the frozen part in a large, temperature-controlled water bath of 100° to 105° F. Experts, of course, tend to find themselves in facilities with just such equipment. That's fine, but climbers and winter campers don't have those facilities at hand. Better to keep the frozen part frozen until evacuation is possible. Walking on a frostbitten foot is preferable to thawing it, only to have it refreeze. Besides, thawed tissue is completely useless; a victim with a thawed foot will have to be carried out.

The best plan is prevention. Keep exposure to a minimum because skin can freeze in the time it takes to zip a zipper. A variety of coverings will protect the oft-neglected face: balaclavas of neoprene, leather, silk, wool, or polypropylene, for instance. Avoid clothing or gear that restricts circulation, such as tight boots or pinching crampon straps. Be careful around heat-stealing metals. Zipper pulls, incidentally, can be sealed in oversized nylon toggles, allowing use with fully mittened hands. Be careful with super-cooled liquids like stove fuels that, if spilled onto clothing or skin, can draw out heat in a matter of seconds. Exercise toes and fingers regularly to maintain blood flow. And always be alert to frostbite's early signs. If you keep on your toes, you may get to keep them.

Snow blindness. It's actually more like sunburn than blindness. Like frostbite, the severity becomes apparent over time, because symptoms can take eight to 10 hours to appear.

Your eyes absorb ultraviolet (UV) radiation just as your skin does and burn as easily. At first, your eyes may feel dry and irritated, then later they feel full of grit. In a severe case, your eye sockets can feel like they are lined with sandpaper. You may not be able to open them for days.

The trick is to recognize situations where snow blindness is likely. The thin air at higher altitudes allows more of the harmful ultraviolet B radiation to pass through your eyes than you might be used to. On top of this, snow will reflect up to 85 percent of that radiation, which is why elevation and snow are such a dangerous combination for eyesight. Climbers and winter campers are prime candidates for snow blindness, but eye damage can afflict anyone exposed to intense sunlight at nearly any elevation. Because water and sand also reflect dangerous levels of UV light, smart adventurers don eye protection even on overcast days. Clouds are no protection against UV rays. Your eyewear should have side shields and lenses that block at least 90 percent of the ultraviolet B wavelength.

Fortunately, snow blindness is not permanent and is generally self-healing. Your eyes will go snow blind before they go blind blind. While the virtual loss of eyesight is frightening, it simply takes time to recover from snow blindness—anywhere from a day to a week. A dark environment and cold compresses ease the discomfort, and patching eyes shut helps in more severe cases.

Frozen lung. Hard exercise on a cold day—snowshoeing, cross-country skiing, or hiking a snow-covered trail, for instance—can cause even the most fit to pant like a hound. If temperatures are low, usually 0° F or lower, severe bronchial irritation results because you suck in cold air faster than your airway can warm it. While no tissue actually freezes, the irritation can cause spasms in airway muscles and burning pain. Increased mucus production causes wheezing when you breathe. Prevention is simple: Wear a hooded parka and a face mask, or breathe through a fluffy scarf or Turtle Fur (or similar fleece neckwear favored by skiers). Treatment consists of rest, breathing warm and humidified air (a vaporizer will help), and drinking lots of water. A severe case might last one to two weeks.

Chilblains. This worrisome phenomenon can appear when temperatures are as high as 60° F. When skin stays cool and moist for a long time, then rewarms, blood rushes to the heat-dilated vessels near the surface of your body. The suddenly swollen vessels can't take the load, so fluid and metabolic waste products leak out of the vessels into surrounding tissue. The tissues swell and become red, itchy, painful skin lesions. Pus can fill the lesions in a severe case. To treat, keep damaged skin warm and dry, and apply ointment. To prevent chilblains, merely keep your skin warm and dry from the start by wearing long underwear that wicks moisture away from your skin and a breathable outer layer that vents perspiration.

Immersion foot. If your feet stay wet and cold, this non-freezing condition can occur. Also known as trench foot, it causes numbness, tingling pain, and itching. Your feet look white or mottled and can become disgusting shades of blue, gray, even burgundy. When your feet are rewarmed, swelling and redness occur, as does intense pain. In severe cases, the skin cracks, and infection is usually imminent. Avoid quick, aggressive rewarming. The skin-to-skin technique of holding painful feet with warm hands is best, but no hard, brisk rubbing! After circulation returns, keep feet warm and dry. Walking may be difficult, so painkillers may be necessary.

Raynaud's syndrome. As winter swirled around his house in 1862, Maurice Raynaud took pen in frigid hand and scratched out a description of the condition that would ultimately bear his name. Raynaud's syndrome results from intermittent spasms in the peripheral vessels of fingers or toes and occasionally the ears and nose. Color changes accompany this painful response to cold; skin usually turns white and often red or blue. Nobody knows what causes Raynaud's syndrome, but thousands suffer from it when the temperature drops. Many treatments have been tried, including avoidance of the cold (hard to do in winter), tranquilizers, vasodilating drugs, hormones, and, in extreme cases, a sympathectomy—selectively snipping certain nerves so blood vessels can't constrict.

For the past decade, scientists at the Army Research Institute of Environmental Medicine in Natick, Massachusetts, have looked for solutions. In the most promising experiment so far, volunteers were placed in cold conditions, then the syndrome-affected parts of their bodies were immersed in hot water for 15 to 20 minutes. With their hands or feet still in the water, they were moved to a warm environment for 15 to 20 minutes. The process was repeated a couple of times a day for several days. Eventually, their brains were conditioned to keep their peripheral vessels open, despite the changing air temperature and without hot water. Stressing that the process doesn't always work, the researchers report that 90 percent of their patients improve, and the mental conditioning may last for years before it must be repeated.

chapter nine:
HIKING
AT ALTITUDE

You've lived and stomped through the flatlands all your days, and now you're ready for a taste of the high country— serious high country, where you can barely breathe and the earth seems to be falling away and the sky has cloaked you in a cosmic blue cape. Up so high it's as though you're on a cloud and can peer down not only at the world but, for one brilliant moment, at your own life. Philosopher Friedrich Nietzsche had a term for these events so clear and insuperable and radiant that they leave a thumbprint on your soul. He called them *eternal moments.* One grand reason to hike high is to have incomparable, eternal moments.

But it's not easy. Nothing worthwhile ever is. And it's not completely safe. Nothing worthwhile ever is. The mountains aren't simple, predictable, or rational. They don't play by human rules. Mountains are the glorious domain of God the inscrutable and sometimes merciless. You want to go up? Then there's no room for complacency or complaining or competition. You want to get back down? Then go prepared. Here are your 10 steps to the sky.

1) Weather. Wild weather is the norm, and wind is the most common problem. It may be sunny and 50° F at the trailhead, while 5,000 feet higher the chill factor is 15° F. Because wind often brings in moisture, if you are serious about hiking high, garments that are both waterproof and breathable are essential. Any garment that's only waterproof will make you sweat too much, and one that's only windproof won't guard against hypothermia if it starts to rain, snow, sleet, hail, squall, or anything else that can happen on an ordinary mountain day. Your wind jacket must have a hood and be baggy enough to accommodate a heavy sweater underneath. Wind pants with full-length side zippers, so you can get them on without taking off your boots, are preferable. Gaiters are a must for snow, scree (rock particles), or mud. Bring a cap that you can pull down over your ears and mittens or gloves that are either synthetic or wool—never cotton or leather because they won't dry.

Up high, the sun is the wind's indomitable companion. Wear sunglasses at all times, add a visored cap, and coat your face with sunscreen. Double the dose of sunscreen for your lips and ears, and remember to plug it up your nose if you'll be hiking on snow because sun reflects off snow and can burn the insides of your nostrils.

2) Ski poles. Up high while crossing streams, jumping talus, or balancing along knife-edged arêtes, ski poles are indispensable. Indeed, except for when hiking in heavily glaciated mountains such as the Cascades, ski poles are far more useful than an ice axe. Adjustable ski poles are the most versatile and thus the most useful.

3) Packs. There's one trick to packing a pack for hiking high: Everything must go inside. None of this cup-or-cap-or-pad-hanging-off nonsense. If it's windy, the stuff will fly around and hit you in the face. Second, on narrow, precipitous trails, gear dangling from a pack can catch on things—krummholz, a glacial erratic, rock walls—and throw you off balance, and perhaps off the mountain. Keep compression straps tight and the pack properly adjusted. Bounding boulder to boulder, you don't want the pack or its contents shifting—you could easily be thrown off balance.

Also, don't forget to bring a spare rucksack for dayhiking after you've set up camp. Not a bookbag but a 2,000-cubic-inch rucksack that can hold a sweater, wind pants, a wool cap, maps, water bottles, and food.

4) Pace. You can wear the right clothes and still die of hypothermia if you don't know how to walk. That's right, walk. You must pick a pace you can maintain all day without sweating. It's called the "mountaineer's pace"—methodical, rhythmic, and inexorable. It's your pace, not someone else's, and it's the speed at which you feel comfortable walking.

Of course, you should take brief breaks (five to 10 minutes) each hour. Long breaks generally lead to fatigue and stiffness, particularly if it's cold. There's an art to taking a "good break." Always search for sunny, wind-protected locations. If it means stopping an extra 10 minutes early or walking an extra 10 minutes farther, do it. When you stop, put on a layer of insulation before you start to cool down. Always carry a foam pad to sit on.

When ascending, take trails wherever possible because not only is it ecologically sound, it's easier. If you have to bushwhack, move diagonally in a zigzag fashion. It's slower but smarter in the long run.

5) Eat between meals. Drink and eat a little something during each break, or at least during every other break. Carbohydrates are preferable. And naturally, keep replenishing lost fluids. You should be drinking two to four quarts a day. Regular old water is still the best liquid you can drink when hiking high up, even if it is dull.

6) Lightning. Lightning storms are a common occurrence in the high mountains. Although they account for few deaths (more hikers die from hypothermia in the rain at low elevations), they are quite serious. The two basic dangers are a direct strike and ground currents. Here are some tips if your hair starts standing on end and the air around you sounds like bees buzzing:

• Avoid wet, low areas as well as overhangs and small caves. Large caves are good, but don't touch the walls.
• Seek shelter in a spot with nearby projections taller than you. Find a small, detached rock, put your pack on it, then crouch on top of your pack, keeping your feet close together and hands off the ground. You want to minimize your contact with the ground but also stay as low as possible. Metal objects don't attract lightning but they are conductors, so don't hold on to your ski poles.

7) Missiles. They have this unmistakable whirring sound. It starts far away as crackling noises, then the whirring. They are the tiny terminators as deadly as bullets. Rockfall! Gravity always has a grip on the world even when you forget about it, so don't. Walk quietly below cliffs, rock walls, and over-hangs. Keep a lookout for missiles imbedded in and around the trail. The greatest danger is when the sun hits the tops of ridges and peaks and begins to melt the snow. The running water subsequently kicks off rocks and sometimes ice. A rock the size of a baseball can kill you if it hits you in the head.

8) Boulder fields. Inevitably, you'll end up crossing piles of boulders known as talus slopes. In many cases, the boul-ders are the size of automobiles and often delicately balanced at the angle of repose. Walk carefully because they're like sleeping dragons. Always hike diagonally across talus slopes, with each person waiting until the one in front has reached relative safety. If the boulder beneath you starts to go, keep moving forward.

Sometimes a slope is a rock slide just waiting to happen. It's hard for the inexperienced to tell if this will happen, so a good rule of thumb is to avoid traversing the middle of the slope if possible. Move along the base of the rock wall, using the wall itself for hand- and footholds.

9) Avalanches. Whether you're looking for a backcountry hot spring or you're just out for a few days of skiing or winter camping in the snow-covered mountains, becoming avalanche-literate is crucial. Steep gullies are clear avalanche tracks. Not so clear are sparsely wooded slopes. Look for bro-ken trees or swaths of forest with the saplings bent over and larger trees with their lower limbs missing. Avalanche-prone slopes will have avalanche debris. Be on the lookout for small chunks to large blocks of snow that look as if they were bull-dozed up in piles at the base of the hillside. Look for fracture lines (cracks in the snow) and actual fractures (down-sloping ledges where a slab avalanche has broken away).

If you encounter any of these conditions, check your com-pass to see which way the avalanche-prone slope faces. Check your map to determine the elevation at which the avalanche started, since snow layering and instability tend to be similar on slopes with the same characteristics and eleva-tion. Using the recognized avalanche-prone slopes as models, change your route.

Sometimes you can see avalanche potential as you ski or hike across small, steep undulations in the terrain. Your added weight may disturb enough of a buried weak layer for the overlying snow to start breaking away. When this happens, you might see fractures shooting away from under your feet. Sometimes you will actually hear the "whoomph" sound associated with a collapsing buried layer of snow. Both of these conditions, besides scaring you to death, are clear signs that you're on the wrong slope and in imminent danger.

Once you identify an avalanche-prone slope, remain above it. Travel on the windswept side of a ridge. Usually the leeward sides are where cornices develop. The slopes below these cornices have accumulations of wind-transported snow that may be overloading buried weaker layers.

The problem is that not all ridges have clearly defined windward and leeward sides because of shifting winter winds. Nor is it always easy to tell which way cornices have been built, especially when visibility is obscured by fog or snowfall. One clue is that a windward side will usually have larger scour patterns as a result of wind erosion.

If you can't reach the ridgeline, stay high on a slope to traverse. Cross the slope quickly one person at a time, with each following in the tracks of the other. When crossing any avalanche-prone slope, unsnap your backpack waistbelt. If skiing, set your bindings on their loosest notch and take your hands out of your pole straps. Companions waiting to cross should watch each person's progress. Should the slope give way, watch the person through the entire descent so you'll have an idea of his location when the snow stops sliding.

As your knowledge of snow increases and you decide to venture farther into the snow-covered mountains, there are a few other essential steps to becoming avalanche-literate.

• Always carry a strong mountaineering shovel, one that can dig through cement-hard avalanche debris.
• Buy or rent an electronic avalanche rescue beacon and learn how to use it.
• Take a weekend avalanche course. Since it could very well save your life, it's worth the money.
• Before every trip, get a mountain weather forecast and

call the avalanche information service if one is available. If not, call the district park or forest ranger office or ski patrol office. Always leave a description of your route and when you'll return.

Avalanches can't be predicted with 100 percent accuracy. Becoming avalanche-literate does not mean you won't be buried. Swiss avalanche specialist Andre Roch summed it up best: "The avalanche does not know you are an expert."

10) Streams. The best time to cross a stream is early in the morning, when the flow is lowest. During the day, snowmelt can dramatically swell a stream. The diurnal pattern of water flow in the mountains is important to recognize. The stream you managed easily at 6 A.M. may be impossible to recross at 4 P.M. Rather than wait until you're on your way down, tired and clumsy, determine a probable "good" stream crossing site on the way in. Naturally, not all parts of a stream are the same. Look for areas that flatten out around large bends, with gravel rather than rocky bottoms.

For the crossing itself, ski poles are indispensable, as are a pair of sneakers or Aqua Socks. If at all possible, try to keep your boots dry. If you have to hike with wet boots, you're likely to get blisters (especially with leather boots). Keeping your clothes dry is also important. Crossing nude from the waist down (except for your feet!) may look silly, but when you have dry clothes to jump into on the far shore, it's worth it. Always unfasten your pack waistbelt during the crossing, and take slow, well-planted steps. Although it's possible to use a nylon rope to aid in stream crossings, if the water is strong enough to knock you off your feet and carry you away, find another place to cross.

ALTITUDE SICKNESS

Some 400 years ago, Jesuit missionary Jose de Acosta described the discomforts he suffered while crossing the Peruvian Andes: "I was surprised with such pangs of straining and casting as I thought to cast up my heart, too. . . . " He guessed his condition was altitude-related, that the "element of the air is there so subtile [sic] and delicate, as it is not portionable with the breathing of man." He was right. Though he didn't know it, he was suffering acute mountain sickness (AMS).

The disorder is a protean one. The symptoms—headache, nausea, insomnia, and loss of appetite, energy, or coordination—can arise singly or en masse, varying in intensity from annoying to agonizing. Onset usually occurs eight to 24 hours after arrival "at altitude" (roughly 8,000 feet or higher), thus sparing many day-trippers but slamming those who spend the night on high. And while AMS is normally non-lethal, individual susceptibility to it varies so greatly that it should be a concern for anyone heading into high country. Hiking trails from Yosemite to Yellowstone toe the 8,000-foot mark, and some Colorado paths never dip so low.

Most of the time, this disorder is merely annoying and eminently manageable. It can, however, turn life-threatening if left untreated. High-altitude pulmonary edema, in which the lungs fill with fluid, or high-altitude cerebral edema—fluid accumulation in and around the brain—can result. Both conditions can lead to a coma and death. Like AMS, they can appear, figuratively and literally, out of thin air.

At sea level, we are, in effect, at the bottom of an ocean of air, an ocean whose "weight" is measured on the scale of barometric pressure. The higher you climb, the lower the pressure. At 8,000 feet, for instance, it's 25 percent lower; at 18,000 feet, it's cut in half. While the air's percentage of oxygen is constant, the decrease in pressure means less push, which means less oxygen reaches the cells that need it. The condition is called hypoxia.

The cold, dry air at altitude doesn't help the matter. Your body loses moisture with every breath, yet you might never feel thirsty. Most climbing guides suggest drinking up to four liters of water a day, but a better indicator than intake is output. If your urine is diminished or dark in color, you may be a quart low.

If you suspect you're being affected by high altitude, performing light activity—nothing strenuous!—and taking deep, regular breaths often help, because they increase your body's oxygen uptake. Aspirin is fine, caffeine and alcohol are not, and small, starchy meals—carbo-snacking—are good commonsense measures.

Crawling into your sleeping bag is not a good idea. Oxygen uptake is poorer during sleep, which is why AMS is often worse upon awakening. This is also the basis for the climber's credo to "climb high, sleep low." And of course, continuing to move higher while ill borders on self-destruction.

Most important, pay attention to the condition. Because AMS often manifests itself with headaches and dizziness, and because the desire to continue a trip can sometimes overwhelm common sense, hikers sometimes disregard the disorder. Listen to your body, not your ego. Listen to your partners, too. A conversation with your friends, what some call "diagnosis by repartee," can point to an underlying problem if someone sounds confused.

Follow these measures and AMS will, in all likelihood, subside without further action. If it worsens, if your headache doesn't respond to aspirin, if your breathing becomes wet or labored, if you become confused or uncoordinated, the only remaining treatment is descent.

A new rescue device, a portable chamber resembling a large sleeping bag with a window, has so far saved the lives of a dozen or so extreme-high-altitude AMS sufferers. Dubbed the Gamow (pronounced gam-off) Bag after its inventor, Igor Gamow, a professor of chemical engineering at the University of Colorado in Boulder, the 10-pound, nylon-coated bag literally takes low altitude up to the victim. The sufferer is zipped inside the airtight bag, which is then filled with air by foot pump. The bag simulates the air pressure found at lower altitudes. At 14,000 feet, the air pressure within the bag can match that found 6,200 feet lower.

In the end, though, there's no substitute for proper acclimatization. Your body needs time to get used to altitude. Staging—spending a day or two at an intermediate altitude—helps, as does decreasing your rate of ascent, but increasing your sea-level fitness won't. There's no correlation between lowland condition and high-altitude acclimatization. As for how slow is slow enough, there's no accounting for individual differences. For some, 1,000 feet a day is a walk in the woods, while for others, it's a tightrope walk. Listen to your body.

HIGH-ALTITUDE FOOD

"Altitude." The word conjures visions of cold air whistling over rocky peaks and clouds swirling overhead as you labor through a high pass. Even if you have all the right gear to travel through such a landscape, the seemingly simple task of cooking and eating can be an unexpected challenge. For wilderness trips in moderately high elevations of 7,000 to 14,000 feet, heights most backpackers reach at one time or another during their travels, knowledge of how altitude affects your body, nutritional needs, and food preparation can make a big difference in whether or not your trip's a success.

It all starts with air. No matter what the altitude, the air you breathe is 21 percent oxygen. At sea level, the huge weight of the atmosphere above compresses more oxygen into each lungful. But at higher elevations, where the air is less dense, the amount of oxygen per breath is smaller, and the low pressure slows the oxygen's movement across lung membranes into your bloodstream. This is why even fit people sometimes do poorly at high altitude. The lack of oxygen makes it difficult for tissues to store and release energy and produce heat.

A string of conditions accompany altitude. For one thing, it's colder up there. Temperatures drop about 3.5° F for every 1,000-foot rise in elevation. For another, the slopes may rise more steeply, so you work harder to remain warm on hills that are more difficult to navigate. You'll find yourself tired without a clue as to how you drained your reserves. You may have a headache, shortness of breath, lethargy, nausea, lost appetite, and feelings of exhaustion.

You might think a good meal would give you energy and boost your spirits. But altitude can straitjacket your appetite, especially during the early days of being up high. So while you sit there tired, exhausted, out of breath, and in desperate need of a good meal, you haven't any interest in eating. Unless you overcome this lack of appetite, your body will start breaking down its fats and proteins for energy, an inefficient process that further drains you.

You can't prevent the conditions that make altitude so difficult, but you can prepare for them. Drinking a lot of water is your first defense. The increased volume and rate of breathing, combined with the dry, cold air, dramatically increases fluid loss. In the mountains, you can lose an additional two quarts of water each day just breathing. Add a heavy pack to that mountain trek and you can lose half a quart or more each hour. If you don't feel thirsty enough to drink much at one sitting, drink smaller portions at frequent intervals.

If you're hiking above 7,000 feet, add an additional two or three quarts of water per day to maintain normal hydration. If your high altitude activities are strenuous (carrying a heavy pack over difficult terrain), you should drink three or more additional quarts a day. If you go above 12,000 feet, guzzle with abandon, perhaps as much as five to seven additional quarts daily.

A steady supply of food energy is just as important. Since your decreased appetite can make this difficult, the next-best thing is to increase the caloric values of your usual meal portions. Mix the basic food components in these caloric proportions: 60 to 70 percent carbohydrates, 10 to 20 percent proteins, and 15 to 25 percent fats. None of these three energy sources can stand alone. Fatty foods like butter, cheese, nuts, and cooking oils, although high in calories, can cause poor digestion and diarrhea if you eat too much of them. High-protein foods like meats, eggs, fish, and legumes provide essential nutrients but require a lot of time to break down during digestion. Carbohydrates like rice, pasta, potatoes, bread, candies, fruits, and vegetables are easily broken down and used but don't provide long-lasting sources of energy.

No matter how much you eat at a sitting, three meals a day may not keep you satisfied. Snack frequently between meals, and definitely consider taking vitamin/mineral supplements to ensure complete nutrition. Iron has been shown to be especially important for producing heat in cold weather.

As if being tired, grumpy, and without an appetite weren't bad enough, cooking at altitude becomes more difficult. Low atmospheric pressure at high altitudes means water boils at a lower temperature, so it never gets particularly hot. In other words, it takes longer to cook things, which can make you even grumpier. You should plan to spend more time cooking and expect to use more stove fuel than usual.

There is one way around this, though. If your group size is large enough to justify the extra weight, a small backpacking pressure cooker will compensate for altitude and reduce cooking times by raising the pressure and water temperature. Decreasing cooking time saves you fuel, too. Two-and-a-half-quart to four-quart pressure cookers made of aluminum work well. Look for models with side grips instead of extended saucepan-type handles to ease packing. Pressure settings typically range from five to 15 pounds; the most versatile cookers feature more than one setting. Incidentally, salted water does not boil at a significantly higher temperature.

For travel above 7,000 feet, choose your stove carefully. Alcohol and butane perform poorly, but white gas, kerosene, and propane provide very hot flames. Your stove's windscreen will improve heat transfer.

Your trusty grocery store is a good source of foods that do well at higher elevations. Shop for quick-cooking pasta, potato or rice dishes, powdered sauce mixes, "skillet" dinners, canned and dehydrated meats, dried fruits, nuts, hot cereals, cheeses, and desserts. The natural-foods section is worth a look, too.

Unless weight is a major consideration, consider dehydrated, dried, canned, or fresh products over freeze-dried. These take longer to cook, but they generally taste better, so you'll eat more. Consider retort foods (flexible aluminum packages of complete, precooked meals that can be heated in boiling water, often available through military-surplus suppliers) or complete freeze-dried dinners for days when the weather grumbles or when exhaustion overcomes the will to cook.

chapter ten:
SIMPLE TRAIL
MAINTENANCE
YOU CAN DO

There are two innocent words in the English vocabulary guaranteed to raise a sweat: "trail maintenance." And they are important words. A properly maintained path keeps you from getting lost in the woods and makes for a safer and easier hike. Plus, well-maintained trails prevent erosion and protect natural areas by confining foot traffic to a narrow pathway. Unfortunately, trail maintenance is usually the first item slashed from federal and state budgets when fiscal times get tight. That doesn't mean trails have to fall into ruin, though, because there are plenty of simple things you can do.

• Improve drainage. This is the simplest, most important maintenance you can perform. Often it involves nothing more than using your boot heel to grind out a channel for water to follow off the trail. If you carry a small shovel like the compact folding types sold in Army-Navy surplus stores, the task (and many that follow) will be easier. Special tools aren't necessary, though. All you need are your hands, feet, and brain.
• Clear water bars. These drainage structures can't do their job if they're blocked by rocks, dirt, vegetation, and debris. Clear out the uphill side of the water bar along its entire length, continuing three or four feet off the trail. This lets water continue draining once it leaves the trail. Pile dirt you clear out on the downhill side of the water bar. This provides support to the structure and keeps it from being washed away or knocked out of the trail by hooves or foot traffic.
• Clear drain dips. These are basically exaggerated outslope areas. Clear out any debris that keeps water from flowing off and away from the trail.

• Knock down the berm. When a berm builds up, the outslope of the tread is lost, and water can't drain off the trail. If the berm consists of mineral soil, simply kick or shovel it back onto the trail and smooth it out so there's a slight outslope to the tread. If the berm is loaded with organic material, or if it's made of logs or large rocks, it's better to push it all completely off the downhill side of the trail. Be careful not to eliminate retaining walls or other trail-support structures when you do this.

• Ever hike a trail that was more aquatic than terrestrial? If it's because of too few water bars, there's not much you can do. Sometimes it's just a blocked stream crossing. If you're faced with a small stream that crosses the trail but is blocked by debris, get in there and get wet! Pull out the rocks, tree limbs, and anything else that's preventing water from moving. Look downstream. Often a log or rock will block the stream below the trail, causing it to pool up across the path.

• Switchbacks are the smoothest, most painless way to hike up a steep hill. These snaking pathways can also be the longest, driest, most jarring descents ever encountered. Consequently, hikers have been known to forgo switchbacks and head straight downhill, creating countless "volunteer trails" that increase erosion and slope instability. If you find a switchback with one trail (or several) cutting the angle between its upper and lower sections, drag rocks and downed tree limbs across the makeshift path to discourage future hikers from using it. Be sure you don't create a berm that will hinder water drainage.

• Volunteer trails are created when debris falls onto the trail and hikers walk around it. Often, just a few minutes of grunt work can remove the rock or downed tree. Avoid creating a berm with the material you remove. Always toss it to the downhill side of the trail. If you place it on the uphill side, it will probably roll back onto the trail during the next big storm. If possible, place the debris in the middle of the volunteer trail to keep people off and let vegetation grow back.

• In high country, try to skirt fragile meadows wherever feasible, especially when the ground is soft. If you can't go around, use common sense to minimize your impact; spread out to dissipate a group's impact, or better yet, keep to a tiny trail that follows the driest path.

• Take rest stops only in areas where your presence will not damage vegetation.

• Never try to move something that's beyond your strength or an obstacle that might roll out of control. Piles of logs and limbs are often under pressure and can spring out in unpredictable directions. Large downed trees, big rocks, steep terrain, unstable slopes, and the like are best left to trail professionals who have the necessary training, tools, and skills.

• Report massive trail blocks and trail hazards or problems to the appropriate land-managing agency. Let them know the distance from a trailhead, junction, or landmark.

• Where the trail crosses large expanses of open ground, rock cairns are often piled up to indicate the route. In severe weather, these stone towers can be the difference between life and death to a disoriented hiker. Rebuild cairns, or "ducks," that have fallen, but not too high—you could create an unnecessary eyesore. Don't build cairns to mark your off-trail route. Too many cairns can confuse other hikers and lead others astray. If you can't find your way without creating a Hansel-and-Gretel-style line of rocks, then stay on well-established trails until your route-finding skills mature.

• With trash, there's only one inviolate rule: If you packed it in, pack it out. This includes "biodegradable" items such as orange peels, which take months to decompose, and food scraps. Never leave paper in a fire pit for the next person to burn. Never bury food garbage because animals will dig it up. If you find trash left by others, pack it out with your own.

• To keep impact on the trail to a minimum, limit the size of groups to six or eight people. Try to hike in the off-season and on weekdays. Consider hiking in lesser-known areas and on infrequently traveled trails when possible.

• Remember that trails are meant primarily for the protection of nature, not for the convenience of the hiker, so keep obvious unnatural construction to a minimum.

The items mentioned here just scratch the surface of what it takes to keep a trail in good condition. Trail-maintenance organizations throughout the country typically get together each spring and fall to rehabilitate trails and construct new ones. There are many volunteer trail-maintenance organizations out. Here are a couple.

American Hiking Society, P.O. Box 20160, Washington, DC; 20041; affiliated with about 200 local trail clubs.

Student Conservation Association, P.O. Box 550, Charlestown, NH 03603.

chapter eleven:
BEAR BAGGING YOUR FOOD

You're not the only hungry animal in the wilderness. Bears are as aware of your food as you are. To save your meals and ensure your safety, hang your food when you're backpacking.

It's likely you can fend off a starving chipmunk, but black bears (*Ursus americanus*), widespread throughout the Appalachians, Rockies, and Sierra, are another matter. Bears are intelligent and learn quickly, and they will eat anything you do. When they repeatedly obtain human food or garbage, the rewards overwhelm their natural fear of people, and they can become quite persistent. If a bear turns destructive and potentially dangerous, it will be destroyed by park authorities. But bears are the park residents, and we are only visitors; it's our responsibility to keep the bears from becoming problems.

The counterbalance hanging technique keeps most black bears and other wildlife from enjoying your meals before you do. The technique involves two food sacks of equal weight hanging in balance over the end of a high tree branch. It sounds simple, but it takes practice.

Counterbalance preparation starts with your campsite choice; tree availability, not access to water or aesthetics, determines the site. You'll need to make camp early because you'll need time to eat, clean up, and still have enough daylight to play the food-hanging game. Try it from the light of a flashlight and you'll need extra-large helpings of skill, patience, and good humor.

Besides food, hang everything that holds odors, such as shampoo, soap, insect repellent, sunscreen, and water bottles containing drink mix. Don't forget to store wooden spoons, the pot scrubber, garbage, and snacks hidden in fannypacks. Leave your empty pack outside on the ground with the top flap and pockets open so the bear won't tear it apart during his search. Store water bottles out of sight, since bears will test any container.

Ideally, the sacks shouldn't exceed 10 pounds each, but on an extended trip, that may be impossible. The heavier the bags, the more difficult counterbalancing becomes. A carabiner helps fasten multiple drawcords together and eliminates knots, which often come loose. The trick comes in getting both bags the same distance from the ground. Weight the bags evenly and adjust their hanging height with a long stick.

After completing your best hanging job, set up the tent a few yards from the suspended sacks but not directly underneath; you don't want to find bear and sacks in bed with you if they fall. Position a tent window in direct view of the hanging food. Your close proximity will do nothing to keep bears away, but it will let you hear them arrive.

Assemble an arsenal of small rocks by each tent's exit—more than a few, because repeated night raids are common. Arrange your (clean!) cooking gear around the base of the tree and on the ground below the sacks as a burglar alarm. The clanging metal should wake you before the sound of food bags hitting the ground does. Put the lightest sleeper by the window or door, and sleep with one ear open.

All this might sound pretty bearproof, but these camp robbers can be surprisingly ingenious. If the branch is too strong, a bear can walk out, pull up your rope, and chew it until the sacks drop. If the limb is too springy, bears can bounce sacks off the end. A mother might even send a cub out to retrieve the loot. If a bear does score, remember that it's your responsibility to clean up the mess.

If it's beginning to sound like you can't win, then you're finally getting the picture. Carla Neasel, one of five Yosemite rangers hired to roam the park's backcountry and educate visitors on proper food storage, says, "Consider hanging your food as a delaying tactic only. It merely buys you enough time to get up and act."

In the high country, the absence of suitable bear-bagging trees poses a challenge. You might try suspending your food sacks over a rock face by jamming the cordlock into a crack reached from above. You could hang it off a ledge safe enough for nimble humans but not clumsy bears.

There are things such as portable bearproof food canisters, but they're fairly expensive and usually heavy.

Individual parks with varying bear species suggest different ways of dealing with robber bears. In 1987, Yosemite, Sequoia, and Kings Canyon national parks adopted a "mild aggression" policy, in which they encourage campers to bang pots, yell, and throw objects in hopes of restoring black bears' natural, human-avoiding behavior. One bit of advice: Never aim at a bear's face because a direct facial hit might provoke an angry charge. Throw to sting, not to injure; then back off to give the bear room.

Grizzly bears (*Ursus arctos horribilis*) are a different story. In grizzly country, food storage is more complicated and crucial. Use freeze-dried food, which has minimal odor. If possible, do not sleep in the same clothes that you cooked and ate in; hang them with your food. Put all food and garbage in sealed plastic bags before loading and hanging stuffsacks. Sleep upwind from your kitchen area and hang sacks so food odors do not waft over you.

Rangers at griz-country parks don't advocate counterbalancing. Since adult grizzlies cannot climb trees—although grizzly cubs can—they advise suspending food between two trees, 10 feet from the ground and four feet from each tree. Check with the National Park Service before venturing into grizzly backcountry for details on dealing with these unpredictable bruins.

CONVENTIONAL BEAR BAGGING

1) Find two trees about 20 feet apart. Throw weighted end of rope (about 100 feet long, at least ⅛-inch or larger nylon) over limb about 17 feet up. Tie off rope at trunk of tree.

2) Toss weighted end of rope over equally high branch of second tree. Affix food bag to midpoint of line with tied loop.

  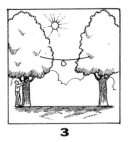

1 **2** **3**

3) Hoist the bag, and tie off line to trunk of second tree. The bag must hang at least 12 feet from the ground.

Bears can figure out that chewing through your line gets them the goodies. A way to foil this practice—at least to buy yourself more time—is to use two lines rather than one, so when the bear chews through one line, your pack or food is still suspended.

COUNTERBALANCE BAGGING

1) Find a tree with a live, down-sloping branch at least 20 feet high, projecting at least 10 feet from the trunk. Toss weighted end of rope over section strong enough to hold the sacks but not the bear—several inches in diameter.

2) Each sack should be of equal weight, ideally no more than 10 pounds each. Tie first sack to rope along with a retrieval loop. Pull it up. Tie second sack on as high as possible, and add another loop. Put excess rope in bag.

3) Toss second sack up so the pair balances evenly, at least 12 feet off ground, 10 feet from trunk, 5 feet below branch.

1 **2** **3**

This takes practice. Retrieve the food by hooking either loop with a stick.

BEAR-BAGGING KIT

The biggest hassle when bear bagging your food is getting the rope over the branch. As repeated tosses fall short of the mark or get tangled in the foliage, patience runs thin. Here's a way to improve both your aim and your temper.

Make a small (4 inches by 5 inches or so) bag of rip-stop nylon, and add a grommet to each side of the bag near the top. The bag will hold about 60 feet of ⅛-inch nylon cord. When ready to bear-bag the food, put a rock in the bag and run the cord through the grommets, tying it with a bowline knot (see chapter 15). Swing the bag around a couple of times and loft it over the limb. Chances are, it will improve your aim.

chapter twelve:
STAYING FOUND

Staying found is a process and a way of seeing things. It's never a remedy for being lost, however, because you don't get lost. You might become disoriented and uncertain, but that's not lost. Lost is what happens to a 4-year-old who wanders away from Grandma's cottage.

Keep the distinction in mind because state of mind is a key to staying found. Consider yourself confused and you can treat the situation with humor and sharpened perception. Conclude that you're lost and you'll start looking for circling buzzards. Let's create a few scenarios.

Case No. 1. You're on the summit of Panther Peak in upper New York's Adirondacks, and you plan to meander over to Couchsacraga. It's misty—it always is—and you're charging through the puckerbrush, paying more attention to the rhododendron branches in your face than the mountain. Before you know it, you're meandering off the north slope toward Cold River country.

Remember, you're not lost. You know where you are because you have a topo map, compass and water bottle—the hiker's trinity. You have many options. You can retrace your steps until you find the slender thread of the main trail, and this time, look back every so often to see where you came from. Or you can contour uphill through the scrub, because you know the summit is up and somewhere behind you. Or you might mumble "The hell with it," sit down, brew some soup, and just wait for the mist to burn off. Or you can fidget around in a cold sweat until you convince yourself you're indeed "lost." (Bad move.)

Case No. 2. You're gliding across Seagull Lake in Minnesota's Boundary Waters, heading for the short portage into Rogers Lake in the southwest corner. The wind is up, and you're driving the canoe into it with a good will, admiring the islands and coves. But you suddenly realize you haven't been counting the points going by as indicated on your map.

Now you can panic. "Omigod, if we don't find that portage right now, we won't make Kekekabic Lake in time to set up camp before dark, and the whole schedule will be shot, and . . . " You paddle frantically past four bays that might hold the elusive portage, eventually going seven miles out of your way when the portage was right under your nose way back there. That's not lost. That's dumb.

In these situations, staying found is more a function of looking at the country you are there to enjoy, rather than abstract navigational drudgery. It's a way of thinking, a way of seeing, and a way of preparing.

It's not all mental, though. There are some bits of navigational drudgery you'll need to know, such as basic map and compass techniques, which you can read about at your local library. You needn't be a topographical wizard, but you do need to be competent and confident.

Next, learn to love maps and to look at them frequently. Share the excitement of them with your companions. Use the map to jack up flagging spirits. Look at it all as part of the adventure you wanted anyway when you started out. And remember, you're never lost.

TIPS FOR STAYING FOUND

• Understand the markings on maps. On a topographical map, the contour lines tell you the geography of the land. When the lines are close together, the ground is steep. The farther apart the lines, the more gradual the slope. If the lines are so close they look almost black, that's a cliff. V-shaped line patterns pointing downhill indicate a ridge; those pointing uphill indicate a valley. Numbers indicating elevation are written periodically on the lines. As you follow the trail on the map and the trail crosses lines with ascending numbers, the

On a topo map, the closer the contour lines, the steeper the terrain. This drawing shows what a mountain shaped like this (B) would look like on a topo map (A).

trail is gaining elevation; if the numbers are descending, so is the elevation.

• There are several ways to orient yourself. Head for a ridge or climb a tall tree to get up high and out of the woods, so you can get your bearings. Look for anything that might correspond to your map, such as streams or cliffs.

• To find directions on a cloudy day, hold your knife, point down, on your thumbnail. Turn the knife slowly and you'll see a faint shadow. When the shadow is thinnest, you've found east if it's early morning, north if it's midday, and west if it's dusk.

• Other natural signs showing direction come in handy. Snow is generally more granular on southern slopes. Evergreens are bushiest on the eastern side. The tops of pines and hemlocks point east. Vegetation is larger and more open on northern slopes, smaller and denser on southern slopes.

• Don't head into the backcountry without telling a friend or relative where you're going and when you plan to return. Make sure they know which local, state, or federal agency to contact about a search-and-rescue operation if needed.

• Prepare for the worst possible weather. When doing research for your trip, see if unseasonably cool temperatures might occur even in summer months. Don't assume freak weather conditions always happen to other people. Carry more food and clothing than you'll need, just in case.

• Get a topographic map of the area and study it at home before the trip so you'll be familiar with the terrain. They're

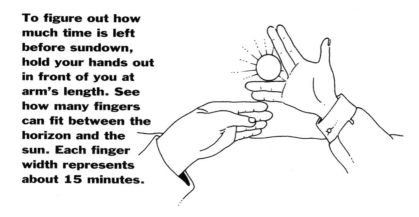

To figure out how much time is left before sundown, hold your hands out in front of you at arm's length. See how many fingers can fit between the horizon and the sun. Each finger width represents about 15 minutes.

available at local outfitters and some libraries. Carry it with you on the trail.

• If you become disoriented, don't panic and start running down the trail because you'll burn up life-sustaining energy. Panic is your greatest enemy, and a positive attitude is your best survival tool. Sit down for a few minutes and calmly evaluate your situation, then mentally retrace your steps. You'll probably realize your situation is not critical.

• If you realize that you're not where you think you are, stay in the immediate vicinity. Wandering will take you farther from your original route, and remember that you left your trip plans with a friend. That route is where authorities will start looking for you.

• If you don't have a tent or sleeping bag, bury yourself in leaves, pine needles, or other forest debris as long as it's drier than you are. In snow, burrow a hole just big enough for your body. The smaller the shelter, the more easily your body can heat it.

• Even if you cook on a pack stove, you should always carry matches so you can start a fire when lost. Fires provide heat, light, and psychological comfort when you're alone and scared. If it's winter and you can't create a shelter, a fire may make the difference between life and death.

• Drink plenty of water. Your body will suffer first from exposure and second from lack of water, which is necessary for mental and physical energy. Your minimum intake should be between three and four quarts a day.

• Signal your position. Bright fires at night and smoky fires during the day can alert searchers. Sets of three signals are a universal appeal for help: three fires, three blasts on a whistle, three flashes from a signal mirror. If a clearing is nearby, alert air searchers by fashioning a large arrow out of logs, stones, pine needles, or whatever is available and pointing it at your location. You can even stamp out an arrow in snow. Laid on the ground or hung from a tree, brightly colored outdoor clothing and gear make visible markers.

• If you run out of food, don't eat anything wild unless you can positively identify it as an edible. Swallow the wrong plant and you're in a world of trouble. It takes three to five days before hunger becomes a serious problem, and longer for it to become life-threatening.

• Carry a lightweight survival kit, even on day trips. All of the following items combined weigh less than two pounds and can be stuffed into a small sack.

Sheet of plastic about 10 feet square for a
    ground cloth
Emergency space blanket. They are packaged in small
    envelopes and tear easily with rough handling or wind
    unless they're backed with the plastic sheet.
50 feet of light nylon cord
Roll of cold-weather tape. Use it to fasten the piece of
    plastic and space blanket (shiny side toward you) together.
    Secure both to the cord and tie to a tree to create a
    lean-to. Face it away from the wind and build a fire
    in front.
Strike-anywhere matches in a waterproof container
Fire starter, which comes prepackaged in stores that sell
    outdoor equipment—or carry a candle
Whistle, signal mirror, or both
Small emergency flashlight
Metal cup for heating water
Tablets to disinfect water
Knife

• Pay attention to your surroundings. It's easy to daydream when walking down a trail, especially if the landscape is featureless or shrouded in fog, or if the trail winds through dense forest for a lengthy stretch. Your awareness can quickly click off without you realizing it. The key is to relax and have a good time, but don't shift completely into automatic pilot. Take note of landmarks now and then, and don't forget to look for that turnoff just up ahead.

• If you're hiking cross-country, or if the trail hasn't been well maintained and is hard to follow, take out a pad and pencil—everyone usually carries one for on-the-trail thoughts and reflections—and make notes. Better yet, draw a rough map of your progress. Include landmarks, both ahead and behind, and travel times between points.

• If you feel like you should mark your trail to find your way back, don't wound the trees. Tie on strips of toilet paper, which will last long enough to guide you back out of trouble. Remove the markers on your way out.

• If you do get lost, learn from your mistakes. Analyze what happened and why. Think about what you could have done differently to avoid getting into trouble. Careful retrospection can fix in your mind how crucial small errors can be, and you may even discover some persistent patterns in your way-finding habits that keep getting you lost.

chapter thirteen:
WATCHING
WILDLIFE

Whether you're a hard-core bird-watcher or just out for a day's stroll in the woods, seeing wild animals in their natural habitats is an exciting and educational bonus to your trip. Here are some general tips on how to find, observe, and appreciate the elusive critters that let us share their homes.

• Leave flowery-smelling soaps, creams, and shampoos at home; bring the unscented kinds. To see animals, you need to smell like an animal.
• Wear unobtrusive clothing and use a neutral-colored tent and backpack. You want to blend in with your surroundings.
• Get a good pair of compact binoculars and practice with them ahead of time, so you can swiftly and accurately locate your subject before it flies, crawls, or swims out of view.
• Spend some time at a visitor center or library to find out what animals live in the habitats you'll be exploring. A habitat is where an animal makes its home and finds food and water. Knowing where to look is as important as being patient about looking.
• Look for ecotones, areas where two habitats overlap—for instance, meadow/forest edges, stream/lake shores, talus slopes/alpine meadows, and sand dunes/coastal scrub. They provide opportunities to see animals from both habitats.
• Dawn and dusk are prime times for wildlife viewing. Some animals are crepuscular, meaning they're most active in the dusk and at dawn (birds, for example). Others are nocturnal and only active at night, so your best chance to see them will be during those darkish in-between hours. In fact, 85 percent of the world's mammals are crepuscular or nocturnal. Diurnal animals, meaning they're most active during the day,

also may be easier to see at dawn and dusk, especially when hot summer temperatures force them to take advantage of the cool, sunless hours.

• Being quiet is the single most effective way to be unobtrusive and see the animals. Take that clanging cup off your belt, and get rid of anything that rattles or squeaks while you walk. Talk quietly. If you're hiking in a group, agree on set periods of silence so you all can concentrate on the sounds of the woods.

• Listen with deer or rabbit ears, a simple technique that increases your audio sensitivity. Place your thumbs against the back of each ear. Cup your hands so the fingers bend over the tops of your ears. Maintain a tight seal around the back of your ears. Turn your head from side to side and up and down. You'll be able to hear a broader range of sounds.

• Pay attention to the shapes and colors of the environment. Very few horizontal lines occur in a forest, so if you scan the trees and see a horizontal shape, it may be the back of a deer or an elk. Look for oblong shapes high in the trees near the trunks; an owl may materialize. Oblong shapes perched farther along the limbs may be ravens or hawks. An oversized boulder in a distant meadow may be a bear or bison.

• Take rest stops off the trail. Animals will often walk the paths, too, unless they're frightened by two-footed creatures.

• Watch the ground because trails often become animal highways after dark. When approaching a muddy or sandy spot, look for tracks and scat. Even if you can't identify the source, tuning in to the animal signs makes you more aware of the creatures sharing the woods. A number of excellent, inexpensive books on tracking and scatology are available.

• When crossing creeks, pause to look upstream and downstream. Rushing water hides human noises, so you may be able to spot a feeding or bathing animal.

• If you see something, don't move! Many times you can prolong the observation by freezing until the animal decides you're no threat.

• Select a campsite away from well-traveled animal routes. Laying your sleeping bag in the middle of an animal trail doesn't increase your chances of seeing wildlife. Instead, the animal may try to use the familiar path, will be frightened by your presence, and will leave the area entirely.

• Set up camp where you can easily observe areas wildlife frequents. Is camping in the middle of a meadow the best way to see the deer that graze there in the twilight? No, but

pitching your tent on a wide ledge overlooking that meadow is a good alternative.
- Don't build a fire. Animals avoid light and smoke.
- Make a "track trap" near camp. Find a soft patch of bare ground and smooth the earth. Check it in the morning or after you've been away hiking for the day to see if animals passed through. This is quite effective if you choose an area that already has lots of tracks and is obviously well traveled.
- Don't turn your nose up at the little critters. They just might delight you with their actions and impress you with their resilience and survival skills. Take insects, for instance. Find a pond or a quiet spot in a stream, and get down on your belly. You may see dragonfly larvae with giant jaws and jet propulsion, or glittering crane fly larvae scuttling about on the bottom, wearing the debris tubes they call home. Insect behavior is as fascinating as that of more familiar animals.

Concentrate on immersing yourself in the natural world. Wildlife watching takes practice, and the more you become part of the environment, the more you'll encounter the wilder residents of the area you're exploring.

Always ask yourself "Will my presence here harass some creature or displace it from its home? Is it alright for me to be here?" There's a fine line between viewing and victimizing wildlife.

ANIMAL FACTS TO KEEP IN MIND

- Pronghorn can spot you a mile away.
- Prairie dogs sense vibrations when you're walking near their burrows.
- If a buffalo's tail hangs loosely, it's not alarmed. When the tail stiffens, the animal is irritated. Buffalo are powerful and unpredictable, so never get within 100 yards of one.

For more information on wildlife watching, contact:

Defenders of Wildlife, 1244 19th St. NW, Washington, DC 20036.

National Audubon Society, Education Division, Rt. 1, Box 171, Sharon, CT 06069.

National Wildlife Federation, 1412 16th St. NW, Washington, DC 20036.

The Nature Conservancy, 1800 N. Kent St., Suite 800, Arlington, VA 22209.

chapter fourteen:
CROSSING STREAMS SAFELY

Only one person could walk on water, so they say. The rest of us have to wade through it, which can be scary if the water is moving swiftly. A good-sized pack on your back makes it even riskier. Learning solid stream-crossing skills is well worth the effort, since the techniques improve your backcountry mobility and open up areas inaccessible to those unwilling or unable to cross a swift-flowing river. You'll no longer be limited to well-traveled trails with bridges and crowds.

Though stream crossing isn't always easy, a few guidelines can make it more straightforward.

• Streambeds tend to be slick, and the bottoms, difficult to see. Even crystal-clear water acts as a lens, distorting the shape and apparent depth of the bottom. Missteps happen easily, and the swift water literally sweeps your feet out from under you, turning your pack into an anchor.
• Before any crossing, make sure you can jettison the pack instantly. Unfasten the waistbelt and loosen the shoulder straps. Put items that shouldn't get wet, like your sleeping bag, camera, and dry clothes, inside a plastic bag. Remove any bulky jackets or shirts that might interfere with swimming. Take off your long pants to decrease the current's drag on your legs.
• You may be tempted to take your boots off, but a cut foot can ruin a hike in a hurry. Most streambed stones tend to be smooth and round, but you often can't see a sharp stick or piece of underwater debris. Also, some snowmelt-fed mountain streams run so cold your feet lose feeling almost immediately. The best bet is to pull boots over bare feet for crossing,

drain them on the other side, and then put the dry socks back on to avoid blisters. When you anticipate multiple crossings, carry sneakers specifically for wading.

• Since three (or more) legs are better than two in swift water, a hiking staff can help keep you upright. It's also great for probing along your underwater path. In deeper, swifter current, the staff takes much of your weight while you move your feet. To get more legs and more stability, add more people. Two hikers holding on to each other are more stable than either could be alone, and a group works better than two. After taking your pack waistbelt off and loosening your shoulder straps, start out facing upstream. Carefully move one foot at a time, making sure you have firm contact on the bottom with one foot before moving the other. Put your staff upstream in front of you to create two points of contact at all times—a much more stable position. (See illustration page 99, Three Legs Are Better Than Two.)

• If you have a hiking partner, have him or her stand slightly behind you, holding on to your pack or arms to make an upstream-facing wedge, with your staff as the point of the wedge. If you are in a group, you can keep adding people almost indefinitely; the wedge will become progressively more stable. To move across the river, have some people move a step or two while others stand fast. (See illustration page 99, The Wedge.)

• Another method involves the "people pivot." Two hikers stand face-to-face, grabbing each other's pack straps or clothing at the shoulders. One person moves while the other lends support. Adding more people to form a circle increases stability. With several people, this system works even if the shorter members cannot touch bottom. The pivot moves in a rough circular motion as it makes its way across. (See illustration page 99, People Pivot.)

• Regardless of how you get across, pick a good place to do it. Finding ankle- to knee-deep water is the most important part. Not only are streambeds usually slick and hard to see, they also vary widely in composition. Smooth gravel bottoms in shallow water provide the easiest traverses, while bottoms cobbled with loose, slick rocks or pocked with potholes present demanding obstacles.

• It's often difficult to confirm what the bottom is like until you're in the water, and the river depth may vary unpredictably. The fastest current usually cuts the deepest channel, which often drops off abruptly. The current normally runs strongest near the center of straight stretches and at the outside of bends where there are no prominent boulders or ledges to deflect the flow. In addition, softer parts of the riverbed erode first, creating irregular holes you might drop into unexpectedly.

• Take a minute to look closely at the pattern of moving water. It almost never flows downstream uniformly, and parts of it actually run upstream in eddies. Even a steep, swift-running stream has some slack water in it, usually near the banks or behind rocks and boulders. Often you can wade from eddy to eddy, in effect crossing several small streams rather than a single rushing river. On larger, slow-moving streams, look for a spot where the main channel widens. The water often is shallower there.

• Avoid crossing any stream at flood stage. Floodwaters carried by even a small creek or ditch pack impressive force, and this power triples as the flow doubles. Telltale flood signs include turbulent, muddy water, a stream running out of its banks and up in the trees, and/or one with lots of debris bobbing along. If the bridges are washed out, change your plans. Camping for a while to let floodwaters subside beats drowning. Floods may be seasonal or local. In dry areas out west, you may not even see the rain that sends a wall of flash-floodwater down the dry wash you're crossing. In the high mountains, runoff from snowmelt flows strongest in the afternoon sun, so cross streams early in the morning.

• Consider what's downstream. Rivers tend to be contradictory, and frequently the shallowest water lies just above hazards. You might have to rule out an otherwise desirable crossing site if a slip would float you into something more dangerous. This may seem obvious, but people die every year trying to wade above waterfalls.

• There are two particular dangers to watch for in forested areas: downed trees across the stream, called "strainers" because they allow water to pass but not floating people, and exposed roots that can snag a foot or an arm.

• Below rapids or falls, the current usually slackens, but the resulting calm pools are also the deepest. Generally, rivers and streams get smaller and narrower upstream, so that's usually the best direction to head when looking for a better crossing site.

• When crossing rocky rivers that are more than ankle-deep, foot entrapment is a concern. It occurs when your foot wedges between rocks, jams into a crack in a ledge, or catch-

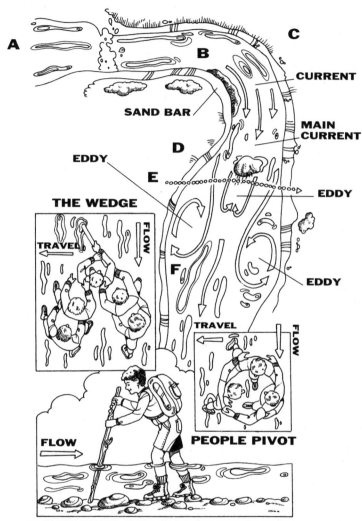

A. Don't cross here. Good shallow spot, but dangerous waterfall just below.

B. Water runs below the falls but probably is also very deep.

C. Water usually runs faster on outside of bends.

D. Where river widens, it often gets shallower.

E. Best crossing is probably here. Wade or swim from one eddy to the next.

F. Eddies: slack water behind rocks or near banks.

es in a pothole. Once your foot is trapped, the force of the current sweeps the rest of your body downstream, making it nearly impossible for you to get free without help. People have drowned this way in water that wasn't even knee-deep.

• If you fall while crossing, do not try to stand back up if the water is swift and deeper than your knees. Roll onto your back, shed your pack (but hang on to it), and point your feet downstream, keeping them up and in front of you. Using a backstroke or sidestroke, work your way to a shallow eddy along the shore and climb out.

• A little advance planning and simple rope work are necessary when dealing with rivers too swift or too deep to ford on foot. You'll need a rope (a climbing rope or 75 to 100 feet of ⅜-inch nylon will do) and a couple of carabiners. The first step is to get the rope to the other side, which usually means someone has to swim it there. Choose the strongest swimmer in your group, but don't tie the rope to him. In fact, neither end of the rope should be tied off while someone is swimming with it; you must be able to instantly release everything in case of trouble.

The swimmer can hold the rope by wrapping it once around his chest, holding the end between his teeth. Or you could use a very loose loop around the swimmer tied with a bowline or other non-cinching knot (see chapter 15). Leave plenty of slack, and have a knife ready to cut the rope in case of trouble. When the swimmer starts, other members of the party should hold the rope out of the water as much as possible to reduce drag. If the river is wide, the swimmer should take a small-diameter line—nylon cord, for example—across first to minimize drag, then use it to pull the heavier rope over.

Once the rope is on the other side, tie the line off about a foot above the surface of the river, and angle it 45 degrees downstream. Make it as tight as possible, using a simple mechanical pulley system like a Z-drag. Then attach a six- to eight-inch loop of rope on the main line with a carabiner. Holding the loop with your hand, face downstream, put your feet up, and let the current zip you across. You've just crossed the river on what's known as a "zip line" or "tension ferry."

chapter fifteen:
10 USEFUL KNOTS

Knowing and tying the right knot can save your food, your tent, your self-respect, even your life. There are thousands of different knots. Here are 10 simple ones you can use on your next trip. First, however, a word of caution. There are two parts to tying any knot: crossing the rope in the right order, and working the knot closed, or tightening it, correctly. The second part is often more difficult than the first. Few knots can be properly tightened by merely jerking the two ends. In fact, there are cases where a completely different knot may result when recklessly pulled. If your knot doesn't work on first tie, it might not be because you crossed the rope incorrectly. Take a deep breath and tie, tie again.

1) Bowline. The bowline is a "loop," or a knot that joins the rope to itself. This is probably the most often-learned and often-forgotten knot; just keep practicing it until you get the knack. The bowline provides a strong standing loop in the end of a line. There is little danger of the knot slipping before the rope itself breaks. It's easy to tie and undo, even if it is wet or has been under severe load.

Bowline

2) Square knot. You're probably thinking to yourself "I already know this one." But also know that the square knot carries with it an undeserved reputation for reliability. It can slip easily if bumped or jiggled, especially if it's tied with synthetic materials or ropes of different diameters or textures.

Square knot Clifford Ashley, the author of the 620-page, 3,854-knot, definitive encyclopedia on the subject, states that when employed as a "bend" (a knot that joins two ropes), the " . . . square knot is probably responsible for more deaths and injuries than have been caused by the failure of all other knots combined." But one nice thing about the square knot is that it lies flat. Its best uses are for lightweight or non-critical applications like tying bandages or wrapping parcels.

3) Sheet bend. The sheet bend (A1 and A2) is the knot that deserves the square knot's reputation—strong and simple, easy to tie and untie, and trustworthy. The doubled version (B1 and B2) is more secure, so use it if something especially important is on the line. If you

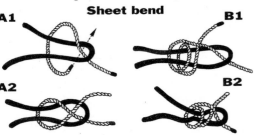

Sheet bend

A1 A2 B1 B2

are trying to join thick or stiff materials, like cables or sheets, use two interlocking bowlines instead of the sheet bend.

4) Short-end sheet bend. This knot will look like the sheet bend, but its special application makes it noteworthy. It will rejoin a broken shoelace when one piece is frustratingly short. The trick here is in working the knot closed. Go slowly and keep in mind what you want the final product to look like.

Short-end sheet bend

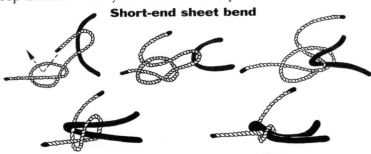

5) Clove hitch. The "hitch" family of knots joins a rope to something else—a tree, a tent stake, a canoe, whatever. The clove hitch is the quickest and easiest all-purpose hitch. It works best around cylindrical shapes like trees or poles and is easy to untie even if it has been under strain.

Clove hitch

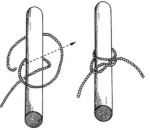

6) Two half hitches. Another all-purpose hitch knot, two half hitches will work around all shapes—circular, square, or odd shapes in between. The "slipped" variation of

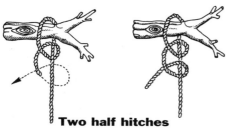

Two half hitches

this knot is particularly important; otherwise, it can be tough to untie. A slipped version of a knot adds a "quick release" modification that ensures easy untying once the knot has served its purpose. Instead of just inserting the working end (the end of the rope that's being knotted) into the knot's final loop, insert a loop. To undo the knot, simply pull the working end. If you tie your shoes, you already know this trick. The final loop you make around your finger and pull through that last hole while drawing the knot tight is the slipped modification.

7) Tautline hitch. Use this hitch when you need to keep tension in a rope that might tend to sag over time—a tent guy, laundry line, etc. The tautline holds in one direction but can be slid in the other to remove slack. It's the best one-way "ratchet" knot.

Tautline hitch

8) Constrictor knot. The constrictor can be used to tie the neck of a bag, say while bear-bagging food or "seizing" bundles of loose material. This knot tightens as tension is applied

to the rope ends but won't loosen as
strain is taken off. That means, among
other things, that it's a hard knot to
untie. Use the slipped version if this worries you.

Constrictor knot

9) Transom knot. This is a
great knot for joining per-
pendicular poles or pieces of
wood, which is useful for
framing a lean-to or emergency
shelter. You can also use the
transom to tie things to a car luggage
rack. Like the constrictor, it's a
hard knot to loosen.

**Transom
knot**

10) The better bow. If you have problems with your shoelaces com-
ing undone and you don't
want to tie a double knot for
fear of having to untie it
later, this knot is for you. It comes
loose with a tug but can't jiggle loose.
The only difference between this one
and your regular shoe-tying knot is that
with the better bow, the working end
takes two turns around the first loop
instead of just one. Then the knot finishes
as usual with a second loop (your
slipped modification) and tightening.

Better bow

chapter sixteen:
A HANDY GUIDE TO BACKPACKING JARGON

Spend a summer on the Appalachian Trail (or any other) and you'll learn to speak the language. If you don't have that kind of time, here's a glossary to get you started.

Access trails: connect the main trail to a valley, road, other trails, or a town. These routes are critical for long-distance hikers who must resupply.

Backslope: uphill slope leading down to the trail.

Bald: mountain with an open, grassy summit that's void of trees. A bald is usually caused by grazing.

Basin: bowl-shaped depression in the surface of the earth, often formed by glaciers.

Berm: "lip" of debris that builds up between the trail and the downhill side. By preventing water from flowing off the trail, the berm causes puddles and mud holes to form on the tread.

Blaze: trail marking. A blaze can be a painted symbol on a tree, a sign, or a cairn. The Appalachian Trail (AT) is marked with two-inch by six-inch white blazes placed at eye level and facing both north and south.

Bleeder: angled depression built into the trail to drain water off the path.

BLM: federal Bureau of Land Management. Most of this agency's land is in the West.

Blowdown: large, uprooted, or broken trees that have fallen across the trail.

Box canyon: canyon with no mouth, per se, that is surrounded on all sides by walls.

Break-in: period of time your body and mind or a piece of equipment takes to adjust to the physical and mental strains of backpacking.

Buffer zone: protective land on each side of the trail that insulates the hiker from activities such as development, mining, or logging.

Cache: supplies, especially food, hidden near the trail for future use.

Cairn: mound of stones that marks where a trail passes through a treeless area.

Camp robbers: any bird that frequents a camp and is skilled at stealing your food. Jays, crows, and ravens are the most common.

Causeway: section of trail that passes through soggy terrain and has been built up with rock, gravel, or earth to provide a permanently hard and dry path.

Chaparral: dense thicket of shrubs and small trees (usually found in the Southwest and Mexico) that survives low rainfall and rapid water runoff.

Clearcut: area where all trees, not just mature growth, have been cut.

Col: pass between two peaks or a gap in a ridge.

Contour trail: "follows a contour," with its elevation remaining constant.

Counterbalance: food-hanging system in which two bags of edibles are tied together and strung over a tree branch. If the bags weigh the same, they balance each other, are well off the ground, and are out of hungry animals' reach.

Cranking: to hike at a fast pace.

Cross-country hiking: to travel across open country instead of on a trail.

Double blaze: two painted blazes on a tree that denote a change in direction or a junction in the trail.

Drain dip: shallow dip built into the tread to drain water off the trail.

End to ender: someone who hikes from one end of a long-distance trail to the other.

Ephemeral creek: one that flows for only a brief period of time.

Erosion: wearing away of soil by wind, water, or foot traffic. On-trail erosion exposes roots and rocks in the tread, creating gullies that damage trees and make for uneven, difficult walking. Off-trail erosion kills plants, creates dust, and destabilizes entire trail structures. Once it starts, it's difficult to stop.

Freshet: sudden overflow of a stream caused by heavy rain or thawing snow and ice.

Full-service town: town near a trail that offers services a long-distance hiker needs (grocery store, restaurant, post office, or bus station, for example).

Giardiasis: infection of the lower intestines caused by the amoebic cyst *Giardia lamblia*. The condition usually occurs after you drink contaminated water. Symptoms include stomach cramps, diarrhea, bloating, loss of appetite, and vomiting.

Grade: trail's degree of inclination.

Greenhorn: inexperienced hiker.

Green tunnel: another name for the AT because most of it is beneath a canopy of trees.

Hostel: a place where a hiker can rest and usually shower. It can be anything from a rough-hewn shelter to a church basement to a home.

Knob: prominent rounded hill or mountain.

Layover day: day off from steady hiking.

Mineral soil: dirt containing little plant matter. It makes the best fill for trails.

Organic soil: dirt containing a percentage of plant and/or animal matter. Organic soil isn't good as filler for trails because it rots, breaks down, compacts, and holds water.

Outslope: downhill slope of the trail. On well-built trails, the outslope is steep enough to let water drain off but not so severe that a hiker feels "tilted."

Pass: narrow gap between mountain peaks.

Pink snow: caused by algae in alpine regions. The algae is actually green but coats itself with a pink gel for protection from the sun.

Power hiker: someone who covers long distances day after day, often beginning before sunrise and hiking late into the night.

Prescribed burn: fires set by the Forest Service or the National Park Service to reduce the fire hazard.

Privy: latrine or outhouse.

Proposed route: unconstructed route that will someday become a permanent trail.

Puncheon: log bridge built to prevent damage to fragile wet terrain.

Ravine: deep, narrow gouge in the earth's surface, usually eroded by the flow of water.

Re-entry: the physical and psychological process a long-distance hiker experiences after leaving the trail and returning to society.

Relo: new stretch of trail built to replace an old stretch.

Rock flour: glacially ground rock that has become a fine, silty sediment. It often causes creeks and mountain tarns to appear milky or greenish.

Runoff: rainfall not absorbed by the soil.

Saddle: ridge between two peaks.

Scree slope: slope with an angle of about 30 degrees that consists of small rocks and gravel. Scree slopes are frequently found under cliffs.

Seasonal creek: one that flows during the rainy season but is dry at other times of the year.

Section hiker: Person whose goal is to complete a long trail by hiking it in sections over periods of time.

Side trail: usually a dead-end path off a main trail. Side trails often lead to an interesting feature, such as a waterfall or wildflower meadow, that the main trail misses.

Skirt: to go around a mountain, often at an even grade, instead of climbing over it.

Slick rock: another name for southwestern sandstone made slick by the rubbing action of sand.

Slot canyon: narrow canyon carved into sandstone by eons of rain and flash floods.

Snowbound: section of trail or an entire area buried under so much snow it's impassible.

Snow bridge: span of snow, often over a creek, that's hollow underneath. Such bridges could collapse when walked upon.

Spur ridge: side ridge that emanates from the main ridge.

Stile: structure built over a fence so hikers can cross without allowing livestock to get out.

Switchback: zigzagging trail up the side of a steep hill or mountain.

Talus slope: rock-covered slope with an angle of 45 degrees or greater. The rocks are larger and have sharper edges than those found on scree slopes, making a talus slope more dangerous and difficult to climb.

Tarn: small mountain lake.

Tent platform: wooden platform used to minimize damage to fragile alpine areas or reduce impact on a heavily used, erosion-prone area.

Thru-hiker: someone who attempts to cover a long trail in one continuous trek.

Toxic socks: a hiker's socks after a few weeks on the trail.

Trail corridor: lands that make up the trail environment as seen by the hiker.

Trail magic: wonderful and unexpected things that happen to long-distance hikers on an extended journey.

Trail name: nickname a hiker adopts. It often has to do with the hiker's personality, lifestyle, or style of hiking.

Trailhead: the start of a trail, usually at a road.

Traverse: to go up, down, or across a slope at an angle.

Tread: trail surface.

Undulating trail: one that follows a wavelike course, often going in and out of gullies.

Viewshed: land that comprises a view.

Wash: erosion of soil by moving water.

Water bar: rock or log barrier set in the trail at an angle to guide water off to the downslope side.

Whiteout: condition caused by thick clouds over a snow-covered landscape. Light coming down from above is equal to the light reflected off the snow, so there are no shadows and no visible horizon.

Yellow-blazing: taking to the roads instead of walking the trail.

Yogi-ing: behaving in such a way that strangers picknicking nearby offer food.

Yo-yoing: long-distance hiker completing a trek, turning around, and going back in the opposite direction, then turning around again.

CREDITS

The information in this book is drawn from these and other articles in BACKPACKER magazine.

J. Michael Wyatt, "Books And Maps," May 1990, pp. 1–6

Carla Neasel, "Spring Cleaning," May 1992, pp. 7–9

Fred Bouwman, Mike Wyatt, Mark Jenkins, and Dave Getchell, "Just Say 'No' To Untreated Water," June 1992, pp. 12–20

J. Michael Wyatt, "Doc Forgey," December 1989, pp. 22–23

Loren MacArthur, "The Perfect Bug Repellent," June 1990, pp. 24–27

J. Michael Wyatt, "Insect Hell," August 1991, pp. 27–28

Buck Tilton, "Beyond The Band-Aid," May 1992, pp. 28–31

Buck Tilton, "Medical Myths," October 1991, pp. 31–33

Susan Weaver, "The Growing Hiker," June 1989, pp. 34–38

J. Michael Wyatt, "Child's Play," June 1989, pp. 38–43

Laurence Wiland, "Dogpacking," August 1991, pp. 43–46

Mark Jenkins, "Beyond The Border," February 1992, pp. 47–50

Buck Tilton, "Summer Heat Illness," August 1989, pp. 51–54

Steve Howe, "Desert Cool," June 1991, pp. 54–56

Larry Rice, "Winter Camping," January 1989, pp. 57–60

Rob Lovitt, "The Big Chill," November 1988, pp. 60–62

Rob Lovitt, "Beyond Goose Bumps," January 1989, pp. 62–64

Buck Tilton, "Winter Worries," February 1992, pp. 65–66

Mark Jenkins, "Ten Steps To The Sky," June 1991, pp. 67–72

Rob Lovitt, "Out Of Thin Air," February 1991, pp. 72–74

Carolyn Gunn, "Withering Heights," August 1989, pp. 75–77

Carla Neasel, "Trail Grooming Basics," August 1992, pp. 78–80

Cindy Ross, "Bear-Bagging," October 1990, pp. 81–85

Buck Tilton, "Lost And Found," December 1991, pp. 86–91

Carla Neasel, "Wildlife Watching," October 1991, pp. 92–95

Slim Ray, "To Get To The Other Side," May 1989, pp. 96–100

Laurence Wiland, "Fit To Be Tied," October 1991, pp. 101–4

Cindy Ross, "Glossary Of Backpacking Jargon," February 1992, pp. 105–11

INDEX

Note: Page references in *italic* indicate illustrations.

If you would like more information about TRAILSIDE books, videotapes, and programs, please call (800) TRAILSIDE or write to TRAILSIDE, 270 Saugatuck Ave., Westport, CT 06880.